Multicultural Nationalism

Law and Society Series
W. Wesley Pue, General Editor

The Law and Society Series explores law as a socially embedded phenomenon. It is premised on the understanding that the conventional division of law from society creates false dichotomies in thinking, scholarship, educational practice, and social life. Books in the series treat law and society as mutually constitutive and seek to bridge scholarship emerging from interdisciplinary engagement of law with disciplines such as politics, social theory, history, political economy, and gender studies.

A list of volumes in this series appears at the end of this book.

Multicultural Nationalism

Civilizing Difference, Constituting Community

Gerald Kernerman

UBCPress · Vancouver · Toronto

© UBC Press 2005

All rights reserved. No part of this publication may be reproduced, stored in a retrieval system, or transmitted, in any form or by any means, without prior written permission of the publisher, or, in Canada, in the case of photocopying or other reprographic copying, a licence from Access Copyright (Canadian Copyright Licensing Agency), www.accesscopyright.ca.

15 14 13 12 11 10 09 08 07 06 05   5 4 3 2 1

Printed in Canada on acid-free paper ∞

Library and Archives Canada Cataloguing in Publication

Kernerman, Gerald P.
  Multicultural nationalism : civilizing difference, constituting community / Gerald Kernerman.

(Law and society, ISSN 1496-4953)
Includes bibliographical references and index.
ISBN-13: 978-0-7748-1000-5 (bound); 978-0-7748-1001-2 (pbk)
ISBN-10: 0-7748-1000-9 (bound); 0-7748-1001-7 (pbk)

  1. Multiculturalism – Canada. 2. Equality – Canada. 3. Nationalism – Canada. 4. Pluralism (Social sciences) – Canada. 5. Canada – Cultural policy. 6. Canada – Social policy. I. Title. II. Series: Law and society series (Vancouver, BC)

FC97.K48 2005   306'.0971   C2005-903213-8

Canadä

UBC Press gratefully acknowledges the financial support for our publishing program of the Government of Canada through the Book Publishing Industry Development Program (BPIDP), and of the Canada Council for the Arts, and the British Columbia Arts Council.

This book has been published with the help of a grant from the Canadian Federation for the Humanities and Social Sciences, through the Aid to Scholarly Publications Programme, using funds provided by the Social Sciences and Humanities Research Council of Canada.

UBC Press
The University of British Columbia
2029 West Mall
Vancouver, BC V6T 1Z2
604-822-5959 / Fax: 604-822-6083
www.ubcpress.ca

For my parents

Contents

Acknowledgments / ix

1 The Bind That Ties / 3
   Multicultural Nationalism / 5
   The Canadian School and Its Debating Partners / 6
   Constitutive Oppositions / 7
   "Civilizing" Difference / 11

2 Confounding Debates / 13
   The Operating Logic of the Canadian Conversation / 15
   Equality versus Difference and Contemporary Feminist Theory / 20
   Equal Citizenship As Unity Strategy / 21
   Reversals through Differentiation / 23
   National Disunities / 23
   Misconceiving the Conversation / 24

3 Just Nationalism? Individual versus Collective Rights / 28
   Individualism versus Collectivism / 30
   Taylor's Procedural versus Communitarian Liberalism / 31
   Nationalist Justice / 34
   Reconstituting the Solitudes / 37

4 Decoding Deep Diversity / 39
   The Meech Lake Formula / 40
   Taylor's Deep Diversity / 41
   A Symmetry at Charlottetown / 43
   Brubaker's Architectonic Illusion / 44
   The Calgary Declaration: Equally Unique / 46
   Rousseauian Dreams of Clarity / 51

Contents

5 Nationalisms Disentangled: The New Treason of the Intellectuals / 55
The Theft of (English) Canadian National Enjoyment / 56
Kymlicka's English Canadian Nationalism / 58
A Conversation Partner for Quebec / 59
The Pursuit of English Canadian Authenticity / 60

6 The Arithmetic of Canadian Citizenship / 65
The Hawthorn Report: From Citizens Minus to Citizens Plus / 66
Trudeau's White Paper on Indian Policy: Citizens Equal / 68
The Red Paper / 73
Cairns and the Contemporary Debate / 76

7 Misrepresenting the Canadian Conversation / 81
Gender Parity / 83
The Limits of Inclusivity at Charlottetown / 84
Difference Dilemmas / 86
Gendered Citizens, Good and Bad / 89

8 Civil Eyes: Seeing "Difference Blind" / 92
Kymlicka, Unity, and the Discourse of the Limit / 93
Taylor's Politics of Recognition / 96
Multicultural Panopticism: From Surveillance to Coveillance / 98
Seeing "Difference Blind" / 102

9 There's No Place Like Home / 105
Are We There Yet? / 105
Home on the Road: Keep Going, We're Here / 106

Notes / 108

Bibliography / 128

Index / 137

Acknowledgments

I connected with many wonderful teachers and colleagues as I wrote this book.

At York University, where I did my doctoral work, I am very grateful to Reg Whitaker, for his invaluable comments and critical eye, and Ken McRoberts, for his sharp insights and generous ear. Other York faculty and graduate students provided plenty of collegial engagement, including Shannon Bell, David Bell, Kate Bezanson, Andrew Biro, Lynette Boulet, Marlea Clarke, Deborah Clipperton, Barbara Falk, Christina Gabriel, Peter Graefe, Les Green, Joel Harden, Andrea Harrington, Fred Ho, Yumiko Iida, Stacey Mayhall, Peter Nyers, Michael Posluns, Paul Rynard, Marlene Quesenberry, Chris Roberts, Christine Saulnier, Sean Saraka, Daphne Winland, and Joanne Wright.

I wrote much of the book while a Canada-US Fulbright Scholar at Rutgers University's Walt Whitman Center for the Culture and Politics of Democracy, where I worked with Joan Scott and Ben Barber, both of whom provided excellent feedback at crucial points in the development of my analysis. I thank as well Kevin Mattson, Karen Balcolm, Andrew Bendall, Susan Craig, Jennifer Gano, Lenore Ritch, and Karen Zivi for making my time at Rutgers so intellectually rich.

I "grafted" several new arguments to the book while a SSHRC Postdoctoral Fellow at the University of Toronto's Department of Political Science. There, Joe Carens' careful comments confirmed his rare ability to bridge Anglo-American and Continental traditions. I also received helpful feedback, and inspiration too, from the razor-sharp students in my graduate seminar as well as other faculty and graduate students throughout the university, including Ed Andrew, Gerry Baier, Sylvia Bashevkin, Ronald Beiner, Stephen Brown, David Cameron, Simone Chambers, Gina Cosentino, Deb Cowan, Kari Dehli, Don Forbes, Rupert Gordon, Ailsa Henderson, Ran Hirschl, Petr Kafka, Nancy Kokaz, Jacqueline Krikorian, Karen Murray, Martin Papillon, Peter Russell,

Acknowledgments

Gabrielle Slowey, Richard Simeon, Dagmar Soennecken, Mariana Valverde, Rob Vipond, Linda White, and Melissa Williams.

Many others provided input and advice at key points; I am particularly grateful to Alan Cairns, whose support and encouragement have meant a great deal to me. I acknowledge as well Ian Angus, Barbara Arneil, Darin Barney, Karen Bird, Idil Boran, Leah Bradshaw, Janine Brodie, Barbara Cameron, Jon Campbell-Luxton, Jacky Coates, Art Davis, Rita Dhamoon, Alexandra Dobrowolsky, Boye Ejobowah, Katherine Fierlbeck, Marnina Gonick, Joyce Green, the late Karen Hadley, Matt James, Will Kymlicka, Brenda Kilpatrick, Kiera Ladner, David Laycock, Kathy McGrenera, Engin Isin, Yasmeen Abu-Laban, Philip Resnick, Daniel Salée, Omid Payrow Shabani, Sue Daniel, Philippa Gates, Jasmin Habib, Shahnaz Khan, Tom Markus, Tom Rado, David Rittenberg, Laurell Ritchie, Bruce Roberts, Miriam Smith, Hamish Telford, Margaret Toye, Peter Unwin, William Walters, and Don Wright.

Although I presented versions of the book on numerous occasions, I acknowledge several especially helpful audiences: at the New School University's Sawyer Series; at Rutgers in the Whitman Center's Lecture Series; at the University of Toronto in the Geography Department's Subterranean Series; and at the Toronto History of the Present Network. Parts of earlier versions of Chapters 2 and 7 appear in "The New Constitutionalism and the Polarizing Performance of the Canadian Conversation," in *Representation and Democratic Theory*, edited by David Laycock (UBC Press, 2004) and I thank David for his detailed comments. Two anonymous reviewers, along with series editor Wes Pue, provided careful and insightful reports, which helped me improve the argument considerably.

The generous financial support of a SSHRC research grant (Federalism and Federations Program), the Ramsay Cook Fellowship for Historical Research (York University), the George C. Metcalf Fellowship (Victoria College, University of Toronto), and publication grants from Wilfrid Laurier University and the Aid to Scholarly Publications Programme made this book possible.

UBC Press is a model of what an academic press should be – dynamic, creative, rigorous, and attentive – and Emily Andrew epitomizes all of these qualities. I am indebted to her for her marvellous mix of patience, prodding, and persistence. I am very grateful, as well, to Camilla Blakeley for the meticulous care with which she oversaw the design and production of the book. In Sarah Wight and Noeline Bridge, I was lucky to work with a copyeditor and an indexer who took the time to understand what I wanted to say and helped me communicate it more effectively. Similarly, David Drummond's clever cover drives home the confounding character of the Canadian conversation.

My family has been caring and helpful in the extreme. Each one of them – Andrew, Anthony, Alex, Bram, Charles, David, Edith, Judith, Matthew, Nella, Phil, Phyllis, Sabrina, Sara, and Simon – has made a difference. And then there is my dear partner, Leah Vosko. In her special ways, Leah helped me make this book a reality, as she discussed it with me on our frequent walks and never failed to support, nurture, and inspire me.

My parents have always encouraged and facilitated my scholarly work, providing unwavering support, boundless enthusiasm – and terrific feedback too.

Multicultural Nationalism

chapter one

The Bind That Ties

> *Between* things does not designate a localizable relation going from one thing to the other and back again, but ... a transversal movement that sweeps one *and* the other away, a stream without beginning or end that undermines its banks and picks up speed in the middle.
> – Gilles Deleuze and Félix Guattari, *A Thousand Plateaus*

> Nationalism is rarely the nationalism of the nation, but rather represents the site where different views of the nation contest and negotiate with each other.
> – Prasenjit Duara, "De-Constructing the Chinese Nation"

Few topics have generated more debate in Canadian politics than the relationship between unity and diversity. Fewer still have produced more written output. Therefore I shall spare readers any pretence of exploring uncharted territory. This book probes the paths previously pursued, analyzing the debates themselves and the charts used to navigate them.

To suggest that Canadians have difficulty agreeing on the character of their political community is to risk being an apostle of the obvious. They disagree over how national unity is best achieved, what it should look like, and precisely what it is that needs to be unified. The Canadian political community is always in question and Canadians have no shortage of answers – answers that are painfully polarized. Canadians often talk as if they have discovered the answer to their national question, but their language has a predictable, almost scripted, quality. Having rehearsed their lines, assumed their positions, and located their opponents, Canadians are ready to perform. Some demand equal treatment of all citizens, regardless of their cultural, ethnic, racial, language, religious, gender, or other characteristics, saying Canadian citizenship must be left undifferentiated, equal, and symmetrical. In contrast, other Canadians demand forms of differentiated citizenship, whereby their differences are not only recognized but incorporated into the rules, procedures, and symbols of the political system.

Scripts like these are performed on high-profile political stages from constitutional and Charter politics to federal-provincial negotiations and in numerous policy arenas. They shape debate over the recognition of Quebec, the parameters of Aboriginal self-government, the contours of federalism, the boundaries of the Canadian Multiculturalism Act, the scope of minority rights, and the underrepresentation of women and minorities in electoral politics. The scripts change, of course, and their language varies, but the oppositions remain: equal versus differentiated citizenship, equal provinces versus asymmetrical federalism, citizens equal versus "citizens plus," individual rights versus collective rights, impartial versus group-based representation, and so on. The Canadian political community is produced through the performance of these constitutive oppositions – through the performance of the "Canadian conversation."[1]

Such oppositions are hardly unique to Canada. They are common in other liberal democratic societies debating questions of citizenship and diversity, for example, the American "culture wars."[2] Still, much can be learned from studying the dynamics of these oppositions in Canadian politics. In a remarkably self-conscious fashion, Canadians have made great efforts to incorporate an embrace of diversity into their national mythologies.[3] Indeed, they are widely perceived to be at the forefront of liberal democratic experimentation in this area.[4] So it is worth examining how Canadians are entangled in these familiar oppositions, and with what effects.

Dichotomies are not exactly in fashion these days, for good reason. They generate limitations in our thinking, exhaust our intellectual energies, and hinder us from pursuing more promising political paths. So it is easy enough to make the case for reorienting Canadian politics beyond the static options of equality or difference, individualism or collectivism, and so on. Who would doubt that Canadians would be better off if they could engage with one another in a less polarized manner? Canadians cannot get "beyond" these oppositions to achieve unity, however, despite their desire to do so. Indeed, this desire is a large part of the problem – or, depending on how one views it, the solution – because attempts to transcend the oppositional character of these debates tend to reinforce them. The unity question that drives the Canadian conversation makes it futile, lost in the very terms of the quest. But to the extent that the Canadian conversation continues, those that participate are at least united in their oppositions. This is the bind that ties.

Multicultural Nationalism

Although Canadians do not agree on issues of unity and diversity, the Canadian conversation is driven by a common set of nationalist preoccupations and anxieties. Rather than attempt to resolve the differences between the opposing positions, this book analyzes the nationalist logic cultivating their opposition. While visions of Canada resting on equal citizens and equal provinces are (or at least appear) incompatible with visions pursuing a dialectic of unity-in-difference, they share an urge to constitute the Canadian political community. Each of the competing positions presents a vision of a unified whole. Yet each vision of the whole centres on a particular array of identity and nation-based categories, recognizing one configuration while misrecognizing others. Should Canada be understood in terms of one, two, three, ten, dozens, or millions of categories of identity and belonging? How should these categories relate to one another and to the whole?

As forms of political contestation, nationalisms are inherently relational; one nationalism invokes and provokes another. The site of Canadian nationalist contestations – the site I call multicultural nationalism – is the focus of this book. I realize that, to many readers, the notion of a multicultural nationalism will immediately seem counterintuitive. After all, multiculturalism (as an embrace of diversity)[5] and nationalism (as a quest for unity and identity) are often depicted as contradictory ideas, reflecting such age-old oppositions as the one and the many, unity and diversity, particularism and universalism. I approach it as a space of contestation, but not in terms of "multiculturalism/nationalism." By my reading, those taking part in the Canadian conversation are all multiculturalists, nationalists, and, not least, liberals. Certainly, they are unlikely to understand themselves (or their various opponents) in these terms: multicultural nationalism confounds the categories of the debate and the philosophical frameworks employed to make sense of them.

Multicultural nationalism is an ambiguous zone. Despite this ambiguity, or perhaps because of it, those taking part in the Canadian conversation are driven by dreams of clarity. The competing nationalisms are concerned in one way or another with the Canadian political community as a whole, and with defining its parts. In what follows, I am not especially concerned to delineate or characterize the various "nations," because doing so tends to reify them in ways that are difficult to distinguish from the nationalist contestation itself. As such, this is not a study of the Québécois, pan-Canadian, Aboriginal, or other "nations," but instead an examination of the nationalisms that invoke and provoke these nation categories. This is a study of nationalist contestation over how these and other nation categories should be defined, how they should relate to one another, and how the Canadian political community should be understood as a result.

Multicultural nationalism is a site of polarization, driven by mutually exclusive understandings of which units of identity – which group(s), nation(s), or people(s) – should predominate in the collective understanding of the Canadian political community. These nationalisms have some conception of the parts and the whole, and so they operate according to a logic of identity. Here, diversity is conceived of as an assortment of different identities, and difference is understood superficially to mean difference *among* the various identity categories. An identity is, in effect, a unit of difference. The logic of identity is grounded in a refusal of alterity, a denial of complexity, in favour of reified and simplified identity categories.

My emphasis on this logic of identity may seem surprising, given the shift away from understanding identities as static and stable, toward more complex notions that emphasize the contingency and fluidity of identity construction. The clichéd charge of essentialism has had its effect, and the now-ubiquitous embrace of hybridity has apparently replaced the identity politics of the 1990s. Rather than viewing identities as unified and coherent, Canadians are now more likely to speak in terms of the interwoven and overlapping play of identities and differences. This understanding is now reflected in the newest "new Canada," the identities of which, Canadians are told, are fluid, heterogeneous, and intertwined.[6] (As if it were ever otherwise.) The issue, however, is not whether identities are static or fluid, but rather the manner in which the Canadian conversation, in its pursuit of unity, breeds identitarian contestation.

The Canadian School and Its Debating Partners
In analyzing the sites of multicultural nationalism, I aim to connect with the growing bodies of scholarship that explore the dynamics, limits, and contradictions of liberal and nationalist ideologies in Canada. A number of important books are part of this literature, including those by Ian Angus, Joel Bakan, Himani Bannerji, Richard Day, Yasmeen Abu-Laban and Christina Gabriel, Eva Mackey, and Sherene Razack.[7] While I focus on the Canadian conversation, there are many other conversations in Canada – sometimes parallel or overlapping with one another and the Canadian conversation – among, about, or in relation to Aboriginal peoples, gays and lesbians, Québécois, women, and others.[8]

By questioning the unity question, and by problematizing the "diversity problem," this book critically engages with scholars of the "Canadian School," defined in particular by the liberal theories of differentiated citizenship of Charles Taylor and Will Kymlicka as well as others such as Joseph Carens,

Simone Chambers, Michael Ignatieff, James Tully, and Jeremy Webber.[9] Taylor's writings have generated widespread attention in a range of scholarly circles, and a growing body of secondary literature exists on his work.[10] He has written with great insight, and considerable influence, about some of Canada's most intransigent political problems. Similarly, Kymlicka has received international attention for his liberal theory of multicultural citizenship. The Canadian School's rejection of the equality script and its insistence on the coexistence of unity and diversity within a framework of differentiated citizenship has captivated a multitude of scholars, students, politicians, bureaucrats, and activists in Canada and beyond. And it has been a focal point of international theorizing on liberalism and difference, such as in recent work by Brian Barry, Seyla Benhabib, Amy Gutmann, and Bhiku Parekh.[11]

I take a relational approach to understanding the scholars of the Canadian School, which means analyzing their debating partners as well, especially Pierre Trudeau and his followers.[12] Intellectually and politically, the Canadian School and the Trudeauites presuppose one another. There is a danger in judging the work of the Canadian School, or appropriating their concepts, without proper attention to their positioning within the Canadian case, and therefore I concentrate on the way their contentions and ideas engage with, and are taken up in, the Canadian conversation. I am especially interested in the philosophical character of the Canadian conversation, that is, its tendency to polarize around abstract concepts. Many scholars and public commentators who take part in the Canadian conversation can be placed on opposing "equality" and "difference" sides. Of course, there is much variation in the positions taken, as well as the justifications provided, with some scholars defending differential (or equal) treatment for certain groups in certain contexts but not others. Still, the differences among those within each group are often submerged by their common opposition.[13]

With the national question on the line, it is tempting to wade into the Canadian conversation and join the debate, but my approach is to probe this temptation instead. This book does not depart from the traditional preoccupations of Canadian unity politics. Instead, its purpose is to understand the dynamics and effects of these preoccupations and, in doing so, to disrupt them. Rather than answering – or even asking – the national question, it examines the urge to do so. And it analyzes the effects of this question, the political paralysis it produces, the exclusions that it generates, and the intellectual blind spots that they encourage.

Constitutive Oppositions

In addition to the scholarship of the Canadian School, I analyze government documents, constitutional agreements, public speeches, newspaper articles, and television transcripts.[14] Instead of focusing on a single case study, this book examines a number of prominent debates of the last several decades. Despite the range of cases and texts examined, the analyses that follow do not aim to be comprehensive. Since hundreds of books and articles are already written on these cases, simply generating more information on them is unlikely to improve our understanding.

In Chapter 2, I elaborate on the central problematic of the book, the polarizing logic of the Canadian conversation. This logic is paradoxical. While Canadians attempt to grapple with diversity in order to guard against fragmentation, they must do this not by suppressing diversity but by giving sustenance to it. While they reject aggressive and assimilative national identities, this very rejection cultivates nationalist anxieties, increasing the urge to constitute the Canadian political community. This urge explains the continuation of deliberations, constitutional and otherwise, aimed at reaching some form of agreement on what it means to speak in terms of "We" Canadians. Efforts to achieve unity in the face of diversity leave Canadians less united. Despite this, some scholars of the Canadian School, such as Simone Chambers, argue that the deliberations themselves – because of their continuation, their inclusivity, and their openness to diversity – serve to constitute a Canadian political community. Indeed, for Chambers, the Canadian conversation is a model for the "new constitutionalism." The paradox, I contend, is that the polarizing character of the conversation serves to constitute not unity but disunities – national disunities. To illustrate the difficulties involved in displacing this dynamic, I draw insight from the "equality versus difference" debates among contemporary feminist theorists.

The next three chapters focus on Quebec/English Canada relations, analyzing the manner in which the Canadian conversation polarizes over rights, federalism, and multinationalism. In Chapter 3, I examine how scholars have interpreted Canadian politics and history as reflecting a struggle between individualistic and collectivist political orientations. Since the entrenchment of the Charter of Rights and Freedoms, versions of this interpretation have grown in prominence, put forward increasingly in terms of a clash between individual and collective rights. I explore this interpretation, especially as expressed by Charles Taylor. Rather than "reconciling the solitudes," Taylor reconstitutes them, and their opposition, in liberal terms by constructing English Canada and its Charter as individualistic. This way, he is able to construct Quebec as different, but liberal in its own communitarian way.

Taylor proposes a way in which the thusly reconstituted "solitudes" may be reconciled, in terms of what he calls "deep diversity." In Chapter 4, I analyze this proposal, exploring competing demands for provincial equality and asymmetrical federalism in recent constitutional debates. The 1997 Calgary Declaration reinforced the opposition. Instead of recognizing Quebec as a distinct society, it embraces the "uniqueness" of all the provinces and insists that each have an *equal* ability to preserve and develop its uniqueness. This position is, of course, unacceptable to Quebec. Each side pursues recognition in terms that preclude the conception of community and belonging sought by the opposing side. The problem with deep diversity, I argue, is that in rejecting the attempt to impose symmetry on all of the provinces, including Quebec, the asymmetrical alternative forces a symmetry on English Canada itself.

The dilemma, for those taking part in the Canadian conversation, is that the competing nationalist conceptions overlap, with many English Canadians insisting on a pan-Canadian nation that includes Quebec as one of ten provinces. This generates recognition claims rooted in mutually exclusive understandings of which units of national identity should be recognized as defining the Canadian political community. In response to this problem, Will Kymlicka proposes an English Canadian nationalism within a multinational Canada, alongside other nations such as Quebec and Aboriginal peoples.[15] As I discuss in Chapter 5, the rationale for this proposal is that it would obviate any movement on the part of English Canadians to suppress or contain Quebec or Aboriginal peoples with demands for equal citizens and provinces, because the three entities would no longer exist within the same national community. English Canadians can (or must) have their nation too. The problem with this proposal, I argue, is that it reproduces the logic of identity already central to the Canadian conversation. The desire to disentangle the competing nationalisms, to provide clarity in the Canadian conversation, is understandable. However, since nationalisms are relational, nationalist contestations cannot be resolved simply by shuffling the deck of categories and configurations.

The next three chapters analyze the grafting of other sites of contestation to the polarizing logic of the Canadian conversation. Chapter 6 explores Aboriginal/non-Aboriginal relations, especially their framing in the terms of a citizenship arithmetic concerned with minuses, equals, and pluses. Here I analyze two major documents of the 1960s, the 1966 Hawthorn Report and the 1969 White Paper on "Indian policy."[16] The strategy of the Hawthorn Report involves supplementing equal citizenship with a limited form of Aboriginal differentiation, which it calls "citizens plus." In contrast, the White Paper, driven by a fear that Aboriginal expressions of difference might fragment the Canadian political community, opts for an alternative strategy of forcing Aboriginal people to develop their cultures within a framework defined by equal citizenship. Aboriginal groups mobilized quite famously against the White Paper, adopting the Hawthorn Report's "citizens plus" terminology.[17] Despite the remarkable changes that have taken place since then, with the Charter and the emergence of Aboriginal self-government, the debate continues. I argue that framing the debate as "citizens equal versus citizens plus" draws Aboriginal people into a set of false dilemmas over questions of belonging and their relation to the Canadian political community, and away from issues of justice and self-governance. As a result, struggles for justice, equality, and democratic governance are turned into problems of the "ties that bind" Canadians together.

In Chapter 7, I examine the debates over gender representation that took place during the 1992 Charlottetown referendum campaign, when the Canadian conversation was at its most inclusive. In addition to the participation of Aboriginal leaders in the negotiation process, the campaign itself included a relatively wide diversity of voices in comparison to previous discussions. Women's organizations, such as the National Action Committee on the Status of Women (NAC), were especially prominent, and they succeeded in challenging the basic norms of Canadian political representation. In doing so, these groups faced a number of what Martha Minow calls "dilemmas of difference."[18] Struggles over representation in liberal democratic societies typically operate according to an impartial/partial opposition. To challenge the traditional liberal premise of the universal impartial representative (who can speak on behalf of all citizens regardless of his or her gender, race, ethnicity, etc.), those who struggle to achieve more equitable representation often emphasize the inevitable partiality of political representatives. Members of equality-seeking groups, differentiated not by choice but by exclusion, are further stigmatized once they gain inclusion because they are denied the use of an impartial voice that allows them to speak on behalf of the people they represent. Their resulting "partiality," despite being imposed, is constructed as a threat to civic unity. This was a problem NAC faced in the Charlottetown campaign.

The mythology of a diverse and inclusive Canada with "no official culture," despite its obvious excesses, has considerable force because it places real limitations on how minorities may be constructed in relation to the Canadian conversation's pursuit of a Canadian "We." Such limitations are interesting since dominant models of liberal citizenship have long been criticized for constructing minorities as prone, if given the chance, to behaving illiberally, thereby conflating difference with illiberalism. At the same time, even the scholars of the Canadian School, well-known for their support for multicultural citizenship, are careful to add a caution to their defense: differentiated citizenship has its limits. It does not mean that "anything goes." In

Chapter 8, I analyze the dynamics of this liberal discourse of the limit, its relationship to the politics of recognition, and its governance of intercultural citizenship interactions. Drawing from Michel Foucault's notion of governmentality, I explore the manner in which Canadians are conditioned to express their cultural and political freedom as multicultural citizens. I situate this multicultural governance alongside Taylor's influential discussion of the politics of recognition. The dilemma, I argue, is that misrecognized groups, in pursuing recognition, must put their identities on display, to demonstrate their "civilized" behaviours. To illustrate, I develop the notion of multicultural panopticism; here, in contrast to the surveillance of Bentham's panopticon, there is "coveillance," where multicultural citizens are encouraged to take part in the mutual study and display of their identities.

"Civilizing" Difference

In this book, I examine debates in the arenas of federalism, rights, citizenship, and representation, concerning Quebec, Aboriginal peoples, ethnic and racial minorities, and women. While not addressed here, similar debates take place over public school curricula, Mountie uniforms, affirmative action, same-sex marriage, employment equity, and so on. The Canadian conversation has a proliferating dynamic.

By pointing to this dynamic, I may appear to be assimilating into opposing scripts struggles rooted in very different histories and political contexts and directed against different forms of power, domination, and exploitation. I may seem to be conflating discussions of legal rights and duties, political representation, and forms of belonging to a national community, each involving different types of citizenship: legal, political, and psychological.[19] I may not appear to be differentiating between struggles aimed at the inclusion of certain groups in Canada and different struggles directed toward achieving greater autonomy for others, such as Quebec and Aboriginal peoples.[20] That the multiplicity and political fluidity of these struggles can be characterized in terms of oppositions such as equality/difference reveals the normalizing power of the Canadian conversation as a model of deliberation. Far from attempting to force these diverse struggles into a single framework, I ask how it is that such a wide range of policies and practices – driven by concerns with justice, equality, and democracy – end up polarizing as they get tangled in unity considerations.

As long as the Canadian conversation continues, Canadians remain united in their oppositions. Through their very participation in these polarized debates – be they focused on rights, representation, federalism, or citizenship – minority groups are "civilized" by the unity-driven space of multicultural nationalism. When political debate operates within this logic, Canadians find

The Bind That Ties

their political categories recognized in certain ways. But, in the very process of the quest for unity, they risk routing their identities into static categories – categories that close, rather than open, transformative political spaces.

When struggles for justice and equality operate within the terms of such oppositions as equality/difference, political choices are structured in problematic ways. The most difficult and pressing questions remain unaddressed, especially where the development of emancipatory political practices and institutions is concerned. The challenge, then, is to pursue struggles for equality, rights, and justice without getting entangled in these depoliticizing oppositions. Rather than attempting to join with either the equality *or* difference positions, those seeking justice and equality are better off refusing the questions that create these oppositions in the first place.

chapter two

Confounding Debates

> Canadians do not deliberate as one people but as many peoples ...
> Multicultural states characterized by deep diversity need to create a
> "people" before they can hope to speak in terms of "We the people."
> The creation of a people, however, must be achieved without erasing
> difference.
> – Simone Chambers, "New Constitutionalism: Democracy,
>   Habermas, and Canadian Exceptionalism"

> The dream of home is dangerous, particularly in postcolonial settings,
> because it animates and exacerbates the inability of constituted
> subjects – or nations – to accept their own internal differences and
> divisions, and it engenders zealotry, the will to bring the dream of
> unitariness or home into being.
> – Bonnie Honig, "Difference, Dilemmas and the Politics of Home"

The defining narrative of Canada is of an unwieldy political project, always in search of unity and forever attempting to constitute itself as a political community. Despite great efforts by so many, the positions of Quebec and Aboriginal peoples within the Canadian political community remain unresolved, as do the situations of groups defined by ethnicity, race, religion, gender, and sexuality. Consensus on a common conception of the whole and, in particular, on the relationship between the parts and the whole, seems always to elude Canadians. The results are a continued preoccupation with determining their common identity *as Canadians* and a fixation on the sources of cohesion that will, at minimum, hold them all together as members of a single political community. For Peter Russell, one of the great narrators of the Canadian story, the problem is that Canadians have failed to constitute themselves as a people.[1] And so they keep trying.

This narrative is so familiar to Canadians that some scholars suggest that it is – in its very continuation – constitutive of the Canadian political community. Whereas Canadian constitutional politics is usually interpreted in the terms of crisis, impasse, and failure, these scholars argue that the deliberations themselves are constitutive of a Canadian "people." This idea has been taken up in a number of ways by scholars of the Canadian School such as Simone Chambers, James Tully, Will Kymlicka, Charles Taylor, and Jeremy Webber.[2] Webber asks, "Are democratic nations really defined by what their citizens agree upon? Is national identity, even in those countries with the strongest sense of themselves, typified by adherence to a single set of values? The answer must be no ... It isn't so much what citizens agree upon as the way in which they disagree that is important. It is the distinctive structure of their fundamental debates – the issues that preoccupy their public life, the ways in which those issues are posed, the kinds of solutions discussed – that give a society its distinctive cast."[3]

Similarly, drawing on Habermas's democratic reworking of contract theory, Chambers argues that even though Canadians have been unable to agree on many substantive issues, they nevertheless manage, through their efforts, to constitute an open, diverse, and democratic version of "we the people." The Canadian political community is continually constituted, and the Canadian version of the contract legitimized, as Canadians deliberate *together* in pursuit of unity, meaning that Canadians succeed even as they appear to fail. Moreover, Chambers holds up the Canadian conversation as a model for the "new constitutionalism" because, she argues, it accommodates and reflects diversity, in contrast to the unitary American constitutional model.[4]

By shifting the focus from the imperative to achieve an agreement on substantive issues to a concern with the process of deliberation itself, the new constitutionalism thesis offers a provocative twist to our understanding of Canadian politics. It is open to challenge, however, on at least two levels. First, the operating logic of the Canadian conversation breeds polarization: to the extent that the Canadian conversation succeeds in constituting a political community, it is a community characterized by national disunities. Second, the Canadian conversation is so "successful" that it proliferates, routing a wide range of political struggles into its polarizing logic, with troubling implications for those pursuing transformative political projects.

To make this case, I begin by outlining the operating logic of the Canadian conversation, where the presence of diversity is, paradoxically, both a source of anxiety and a distinctive basis for the Canadian political identity. I then illustrate the polarizing effects of the Canadian conversation and its imperative to unity: the Canadian conversation, I argue, is a breeding ground for mutually reinforcing nationalist and identity-based recognition struggles. In the manner described by Bonnie Honig in the epigraph, the Canadian conversation always fails in its dreams of returning home, yet succeeds to the extent that it "civilizes" Canadians, especially those struggling for justice and equality, into dreaming of a Canadian home space, a central feature of the ideological site I call multicultural nationalism.

The Operating Logic of the Canadian Conversation

The Canadian conversation is, like most deliberative processes, driven by multiple disagreements. At the same time, it presupposes an operating logic, which participants implicitly agree to simply by taking part. This logic defines the broad objective of the conversation and sets down rules and limits on how that objective may be reached, what can and cannot be said, and so on.[5] Much of what follows in this section will seem obvious, which is precisely the point: in this overcoded field, it helps to begin by defamiliarizing the obvious.

Let me emphasize that the Canadian conversation is not limited to formal constitutional negotiations but instead emerges in a range of high-profile political arenas. Furthermore, while the logic of the conversation approximates the preoccupations and anxieties of many Canadians, it is not synonymous with them in any aggregate sense; instead, it is driven primarily by majoritarian concerns (understood very fluidly)[6] and becomes "common" only as the participants, through their participation, embrace or acknowledge the logic in their different ways. Some obviously challenge or reject the logic of the conversation (even though their presence may be crucial to it, for example, Québécois separatists);[7] others are indifferent to its concerns; while still others are excluded from the conversation altogether. With these clarifications in mind, I present my reading of the operating logic of the Canadian conversation, focusing on four overlapping features: the imperative to unity, anxiety over diversity, the embrace of diversity, and the pursuit of identity through diversity.

The Unity Imperative
To begin with, and most obvious of all, those engaged in the Canadian conversation know what the conversation is about, in a broad sense: unity. Unity requires some form of agreement on what constitutes the Canadian political community – agreement on what it means for Canadians to use the word "we." I will return to this unity imperative below.

The Diversity Challenge
The Canadian conversation rarely strays far from the topic of diversity, since diversity must be dealt with in order to achieve unity. The question, then, is

how can Canadians achieve and maintain unity *despite* all their diversity? While the language varies considerably, the logic remains: diversity represents a challenge (or dilemma, problem, or threat, etc.) to the unity (or stability, harmony, peace, or existence, etc.) of the country (or nation, community, or people, etc.) because it always has the potential to produce division (or dissent, conflict, antagonism, or violence, etc.). Thus for the Canadian conversation to succeed, it must deal with (or manage, attend to, neutralize, resolve, or reconcile, etc.) Canada's diversity challenge.

The fact that the Canadian conversation approaches diversity as a challenge is hardly extraordinary in itself. Still, the diversity challenge plays an especially central role in the Canadian conversation, given the prevailing sense that Canada's diversity is distinctively challenging in both its form (with large French-speaking and Aboriginal minorities) and its extent (as diverse as any other country).

The Embrace of Diversity

While the Canadian conversation is premised on a distinctively Canadian challenge of diversity, it also presumes a distinctively Canadian response, which involves some form of embrace of diversity rather than an attempt to assimilate it. This response entails a rejection of demands for uniformity and of the assimilationist notion that in order to live together Canadians must all be the same.

The Canadian conversation often depicts the accommodation of diversity as having deep roots in Canadian history, such as with the choice of federalism. While it often acknowledges that Canadian history is marked by numerous episodes of racism and exclusion, it tends to view this history as a narrative of liberal progress, in which the accommodation and recognition of diversity have widened steadily.[8] The defining moments in this historical narrative are the rejections of various assimilationist policy proposals, such as the 1839 Durham Report and the 1969 White Paper on Indian policy, which I discuss in Chapter 6.[9] The explicitly antiassimilationist character of the Canadian conversation suggests a political culture of considerable liberal tolerance, but the conversation often embraces diversity in a self-consciously forward manner that moves beyond the detachment and reserve characteristic of liberal toleration; the recognition and the accommodation of diversity are *themselves* frequently celebrated.

Consider the language of the Calgary Declaration of 1997, the most recent quasi-constitutional proposal (which I discuss further in Chapter 4). Agreed to by all of the English Canadian premiers and territorial leaders (i.e., all the premiers except for Lucien Bouchard, then premier of Quebec), it states, "Canada's gift of diversity includes Aboriginal peoples and cultures, the vitality of the English and French languages and a multicultural citizenry drawn from all parts of the world."[10] One does not *tolerate* a gift; one celebrates it.

To be clear, this approach to dealing with diversity as a gift is necessarily a majoritarian discourse (in this case, English Canadian), even if it is often internalized and expressed by minorities themselves. Given its emphasis on unity, on keeping all of the parts together, the Canadian conversation must attempt to constitute the political community in inclusive terms. The results are inevitably troubled, however, since the challenge of diversity is premised on a threatening other, no matter how this other is embraced and celebrated.

Even while it constructs minorities as threatening to the political community, the embrace of diversity entails the exclusion of explicitly racist, xenophobic, or otherwise antidiversity discourses from the Canadian conversation. Canadians may not yet know what it means to be Canadian, but, as far as the Canadian conversation goes, to be antidiversity is to be un-Canadian. Those wary of the diversity embrace must, at minimum, disguise their arguments in acceptable language or risk being marginalized from the conversation.

Identity in Nonidentity

The embrace of diversity complicates the attempt to construct a common national identity, since there can be no explicit resort to a culturally, religiously or ethnically defined national identity. This is a familiar contemporary dilemma, as the British theorist Bhiku Parekh explains: "A shared sense of national identity is necessary but also potentially dangerous, a force for both unity and division, a condition for the community's cohesion and reproduction which can also alienate large sections of its citizens and become a cause of its fragmentation."[11] Parekh argues that it is necessary to centre the national identity on the political structure while ensuring that it is open to multiple identities and forms of belonging and that each member of the community is valued equally. In much the same way, although those participating in the Canadian conversation are preoccupied with metaquestions of national identity, their approach to them is, given their own diversity, necessarily subject to limitations. The Canadian conversation, although typical in its concern with national identity and diversity, is distinctive (or at least often assumes as much) in pursuing the solution *in* the problem by grounding national identity in diversity itself. Who are "we" Canadians? "We" are diverse!

While this approach may appear to resolve Parekh's problem, in practice it perpetuates it. On the one hand, the Canadian political identity must remain, at least in appearance, empty of content, except for the embrace of diversity itself.[12] As a result, the path of *not* creating – or at least not imposing – a singular overarching identity is the defining feature of the Canadian political identity.[13] On the other hand, even if the Canadian political identity is limited to its nonidentity, Canadians remain interested in giving content to it in a manner that all can agree to. The Canadian conversation continually seeks a national political identity even as it is forced to reject the basic identity premise of traditional nationalist ideologies. As a result, Canadians are a political community in process, failing necessarily to actualize their desire to be imagined, except insofar as they keep trying.

The Unity Imperative (Continued)
The quest for identity in nonidentity cultivates even greater anxiety over the basis for national cohesion. It is necessary to determine how the various parts relate to one another, and to the whole, and especially how these parts will be kept together in the form of a whole. The American scholar Arthur Schlesinger Jr. puts the problem this way: "One reason why Canada, despite all its advantages, is so vulnerable to schism is that, as Canadians freely admit, their country lacks such a unique national identity. Attracted variously to Britain, France, and the United States, inclined for generous reasons to a policy of official multiculturalism, Canadians have never developed a strong sense of what it is to be a Canadian."[14]

His assessment may not be entirely fair – this approach appears to be distinctive, given the international attention that it has received.[15] At the same time, the Canadian conversation is consumed by fears of fragmentation and, indeed, fears over the very continuation of the Canadian political community. Diversity is at once the basis for the Canadian political identity and the preeminent threat to Canada as a single political community. This leads to a search for some form of cement strong enough to bind Canadians together and thus guard against fragmentation, but not so strong that diversity itself is assimilated. Consequently, Canadian history has often been read as an ongoing search for the cement of the Canadian political community and, in particular, as a series of struggles over what that cement should look like, how it should operate, and how powerful it should be.[16]

This concern with cementing diversity together, while familiar to Canadians, has emerged as one of the major problematics of contemporary social and political theory. Consider Jürgen Habermas's formulation: "[The] notion of constitutional patriotism appears to many observers to represent too weak a bond to hold together complex societies. The question then becomes even more urgent: under what conditions can a liberal political culture provide a sufficient cushion to prevent a nation of citizens, which can no longer rely on ethnic associations, from dissolving into fragments?"[17]

Reflecting Habermas's question, Chambers insists, "In giving up a unitary vision, however, we should not give up the goal of unity. Constitutional negotiations and dialogue is still about speaking as 'We the people.'"[18] It is worth investigating what this insistence on the goal of unity entails. Even if all those taking part in the Canadian conversation agree that Canada's diversity, along with the embrace of that diversity, is a defining feature of the Canadian political community, they are still driven to achieve unity, which entails agreeing on what that embrace of diversity actually means. It is here that the Canadian conversation reaches an impasse.

For the scholars who favour the Canadian conversation, the main issue is not that unity be achieved, especially in a formal constitutional sense, but that, where it is not achieved, it be continually sought. They argue that Canadians are constituted by their preoccupation with the "we" question, the procedures that they employ in their deliberations, and the manner in which they disagree over the answers. The central tension in this approach is that the logic of the Canadian conversation, in its very continuation, holds the parts together even while cultivating their division. It keeps Canadians dis/unified – together in disunity. I am doubtful that these scholars would view the resulting "we" (divided, but held together) as a legitimate basis for political community, and that Canada has held together in this way is partly a matter of luck, given the extremely close result of the 1995 Quebec referendum. Still, my concerns lie elsewhere.

Thus far, I have described the logic *common* to the Canadian conversation. Its disagreements are varied, but contestation clusters around the question: How are the various manifestations of diversity to be understood and recognized, in relation both to one another and to the Canadian political community? Achieving an agreement on the configuration of the parts and the whole(s) – whether in a constitutional text or otherwise – is the central test of unity and the perennial aim of the Canadian conversation. Not surprisingly, there are a number of possible configurations, each of which places greater emphasis on some parts more than others. Different visions are to be expected; the difficulty is that these visions are so polarized. This polarizing dynamic defines the Canadian conversation.

The Canadian conversation moves far beyond the realm of formal constitutional negotiations or questions concerning Quebec and its place in the federation. Many other sites of contestation – such as those related to Aboriginal peoples, ethnicity, race, religion, gender, and sexuality – are drawn into the logic of the conversation, often framed in similarly polarized language (individual/collective, liberal/communitarian, equality/difference, citizens equal/citizens plus, impartial/partial, and so forth). Because Canadians have not succeeded in constituting themselves as a single "people," but continue to try, all of their democratic deliberations, but especially those involving their diversity, have the potential to get caught up in the unity question.

Such deliberations are then faced with the impossible task of trying to answer it, breeding nationalist and identitarian contestation. This is not to suggest that the logic of the Canadian conversation dominates all democratic deliberations, only that it has the *potential* to dominate any arena of deliberation at any given moment.

Equality versus Difference and Contemporary Feminist Theory

Equality and difference are often presented in scholarly discourse as dichotomous, as if they represent two mutually exclusive sets of political, social, cultural, or economic choices. Dichotomies present two terms in a static either/or scenario, without middle ground. Lorraine Code explains, "Dichotomies are especially problematic in that they posit exclusionary constructs, not complementary or interdependent ones that could shade into one another or function as 'mixed modes' rather than absolutes. In dichotomous thinking the opposed terms are like Aristotelian contradictories, which must conform to the principle of the excluded middle. Everything has to be *either* A *or* Not-A, for A and Not-A exhaust all possibilities. Continuity between the terms is a logical impossibility."[19]

The equality/difference dichotomy has been a focus of analysis in several streams of contemporary social and political thought, especially within feminist theory.[20] Indeed, some feminist theorists suggest that the history of feminism has been driven by a disagreement over whether to strive to achieve equality with men, where this means equal citizenship, or whether to reject this form of equality as inevitably imbued with masculine norms, and instead struggle to ensure that women's differences are acknowledged and valued. For example, Nancy Fraser has traced the manner in which the equality and difference positions in US feminist debates have each evolved in relation to the other. While she believes that the evolution of these dichotomous positions has moved feminist theory forward in a generally positive direction, the failure to resolve these debates has left US feminism "with a truncated problematic." Fraser's alternative is not to dismiss the dichotomous character of these debates but rather to "construct a new equality/difference debate, one oriented to multiple intersecting differences."[21] This would allow, she argues, a reconstruction of struggles for cultural recognition that, because they tend to emphasize difference, contradict equally important struggles for socioeconomic justice, which emphasize equality. Fraser's reframing of the equality/difference dichotomy in terms of a distinction between economics (or redistribution) and culture (or recognition) has been the subject of vigorous debate.[22] Interestingly, Fraser is not unlike Charles Taylor in making this distinction, although Taylor's focus is on the difference, culture, and recognition side of the dichotomy. In contrast, Fraser argues that the main task is to reject taking one side or the other and instead to develop a mutually reinforcing relationship between the cultural and economic spheres, which would involve more radical approaches in each.

Fraser attempts to build emancipatory strategies upon the logic of dichotomies such as economy/culture, redistribution/recognition, or equality/difference. Far more promising are those feminist theorists who refuse to operate within the terms of the equality/difference dichotomy, pursuing instead deconstructive strategies that problematize the dichotomy itself. Especially notable here is Joan W. Scott, who argues,

> When equality and difference are paired dichotomously, they structure an impossible choice. If one opts for equality, one is forced to accept the notion that difference is antithetical to it. If one opts for difference, one admits that equality is unattainable ... Feminists cannot give up "difference"; it has been our most creative analytic tool. We cannot give up equality, at least as long as we want to speak to the principles and values of a democratic political system. But it makes no sense for the feminist movement to let its arguments be forced into pre-existing categories, its political disputes be characterized by a dichotomy we did not invent.[23]

Scott maintains that the tendency to read feminist history in the terms of equality/difference, as Fraser and many others do, actually reinforces the static play of the dichotomy. Only by displacing the equality/difference dichotomy can we reorient these concepts so that they are no longer opposed but mutually reinforcing. According to Scott, "Instead of framing analyses and strategies as if such binary pairs were timeless and true, we need to ask how the dichotomous pairing of equality and difference itself works."[24] In what follows, I pursue this line of questioning, drawing insight from feminist theorizing as well as others who have employed similar strategies. The oppositions of the Canadian conversation, however – and thus the strategies I employ in analyzing them – each have their own distinctive dynamics.

Equal Citizenship As Unity Strategy

Despite the tendency of dichotomies to heighten the distinctiveness of the two opposed terms, each term exists in a mutually dependent relationship with the other. Scott illustrates this rather well, saying that equality "presumes a social agreement to consider obviously different people as equivalent (not identical) for a stated purpose ... The political notion of equality thus includes, indeed depends on, an acknowledgment of the existence of difference. Demands for equality have rested on implicit and usually unrecognized arguments from difference; if all individuals or groups were identical or the same there would be no need to ask for equality. Equality might well be defined as deliberate indifference to specified difference."[25] Within the terms of the opposition, equality exists to annul certain differences, even while it derives its meaning from the presence of difference. In this way, equality attempts to negate in certain respects its own condition of existence, difference.

What does this mutual yet hierarchical reliance between equality and difference tell us about the oppositions of the Canadian conversation? Here, equality strategies operate on certain differences in order to construct a basis for Canadian unity. The vigour with which so many Canadians pursue equality demonstrates their anxiety about the wide-ranging and multiple play of differences in Canada, without which there would be no impetus for their equality position.

However, what are we to make of the demand for equality in conjunction with the preservation and even celebration of diversity? That is, if equality strategies have the purpose of *suppressing* difference, how is it that equality and diversity are usually presented together, as if mutually reinforcing? The answer lies in the distinct meanings of diversity and difference as they are used in the Canadian conversation. As I described it above, the Canadian conversation is driven by the threat that diversity, as a source of fragmentation and division, represents for Canadian unity. Instead of attempting to eliminate diversity through assimilationist policies, the Canadian conversation is premised on managing and even celebrating diversity so that it is directed toward the ends of unity. In this context, equality defines the space within which diversity can "safely" play out.

For some, this threat to unity is exacerbated when diversity is manifested as asymmetrical difference or differentiation. While diversity can be directed toward unity, difference is understood as a reflection of fragmentation and disunity. Equality strategies aim to control such differences, an example being the equality of citizens and provinces demanded by Trudeau and the old Reform/Canadian Alliance parties, directed at containing Quebec, Aboriginal peoples, and others.

These equality strategies are not necessarily individualistic, although they are often put forward or rejected as if they were. Instead, depending on the context and the differences in play, equality strategies may operate in relation to a number of groupings or units, such as citizens, provinces, languages, or religions. Whatever the units, equality strategies emphasize their symmetry. Rather than eliminate the differences among the units, equality strategies normalize them in some form of symmetrical pattern. They standardize certain aspects of how Canadians, or groups of Canadians, belong to the Canadian political community.

Reversals through Differentiation

In response to these equality strategies, the Canadian conversation polarizes as a range of difference strategies are pursued. In opposition to the uniform or symmetrical basis of belonging, there is now acknowledgment and even encouragement of differences in the relationships between citizens and the Canadian political community. Quebec, Aboriginal peoples, and other communities assert their differences in opposition to the idea of equality as symmetry. They reject equal citizenship in favour of differentiated citizenship, asymmetrical federalism, a distinct society clause, Aboriginal self-government, affirmative action, group-based representation, and so on. These and other difference strategies have been defended in various ways by the scholars of the Canadian School, including Will Kymlicka's theory of multicultural citizenship, James Tully's idea of the recognition of cultural diversity, and Charles Taylor's notion of "deep diversity."[26]

As varied as these practices and theories of differentiated citizenship are, they share a rejection of some form of uniformity, symmetry, or equal treatment and they represent important reversals of the oppositions of the Canadian conversation, especially given the hierarchical power relations involved. While such reversals are necessary, the polarizing logic of the opposition must be displaced altogether so that the newly valued term – some form of difference – is no longer placed in an oppositional role to equality.

National Disunities

Rather than give up on either term of the dichotomy, it is necessary to displace them, to dissolve their opposition.[27] This occurs not by demanding (or theorizing) difference in opposition to equality but, as Scott says, by viewing "differences as the very meaning of equality itself."[28] This alternative is pre-empted by the terms of the Canadian conversation, where struggles around difference are fed back into the same logic, leaving Canadians with political choices that are rigidly polarized. In opposition to the symmetrical units of equality, the drive for difference is transformed into a form of identity politics. Difference itself becomes totalizing and uniform in its oppositional stance toward equality. A category of difference, such as Quebec, Aboriginal peoples, or English Canada, becomes essentialized and standardized in the form of a "nation" or some other category, which is then put forward in totalizing identitarian terms. Instead of the dichotomy being displaced, the struggles over symmetry and uniformity are reproduced *within* the differentiated category. As a result, in response to the fundamentalist flavour of the equality discourse, the difference discourse begins to take on its own fundamentalist flavour.

Why do these difference strategies often fail to displace the opposition and instead become congealed in the form of an essentialist and totalizing identity politics? On the one hand, the attempt to achieve unity through equality implies difference, and generates a response from difference. The imposition of equality, of a layer of uniformity, necessarily and by design suppresses heterogeneity and complexity. Even though space is made for a degree of diversity, the attempt to cultivate unity through a layer of uniformity fails. According to Bonnie Honig, difference "resists or exceeds the closure of identity. It signals not a difference *from* others but a difference that troubles identity from with*in* its would-be economy of the same. Difference is what identity perpetually seeks (and fails) to expunge, fix, or hold in place. In short, difference is a problem for identity, not one of its adjectives."[29]

On the other hand, the pursuit of difference – in opposition to the imposition of unity through equality – generates distinct categories of difference, or units of difference, through which this opposition is expressed. It is not long before the search begins for the authentic identity of each unit of difference, a search that generates yet another set of exclusions and suppresses the internal heterogeneity and complexity of each category of difference. In their opposition to a uniform basis of belonging, in their quest for a politics that breaks free of the shallow diversity found in the multicultural mosaic, those pursuing difference find themselves insisting upon another basis of unity, another layer of uniformity. The unity imperative, the fear of diversity and fragmentation, generates multiple and competing unities and subunities. This is the impasse to which the logic of the Canadian conversation leads – not to unity but to disunities.

Misconceiving the Conversation
To be sure, the scholars of the Canadian School are well aware of the polarized character of the Canadian conversation. According to Jeremy Webber, "It sometimes seems that we are caught between two poles: either all groups should get special consideration or none should. We may be tempted to follow the Reform Party's approach, avoiding the problem altogether by treating all identically."[30] Despite this awareness, the polarized pattern that I have been describing is obviously not what Webber has in mind when he points to the ways in which Canadians disagree as constitutive of the Canadian community. Although it may not please Webber, these polarizing oppositions are

a dominant feature of the Canadian conversation and, therefore, by his own definition, they serve to constitute the Canadian political community. Furthermore, this result is not coincidental: it is *because* the Canadian conversation aims for *agreement* on the character of the Canadian political community that it has these divisive effects.

Much like Webber, Kenneth McRoberts characterizes those who operate according to the equal citizens and equal provinces model, such as Trudeau and his followers, as "misconceiving" Canada.[31] This implies that there is a correct conception of the Canadian political community – whether rooted in Canadian history or otherwise "out there" – that need only be grasped. However, the real misconception lies in the operating logic of the Canadian conversation itself, with the premise that the Canadian political community must be conceived and, furthermore, that this must be done in a manner with which Canadians can agree. *Any* attempt to conceive of Canada, however inclusive of diversity, will generate counterconceptions.

Of the scholars of the Canadian School, James Tully alone seems to have come to an understanding along these lines. He characterizes the impasse as a problem of "diversity blindness" in which everyone continues to look at, and judge, the various proposals only through his or her own "federation story," a kind of language game based on different "modes or ways of experiencing Canada, of being Canadian."[32] The problem is that Canadians negotiate from the perspective of these diverse federation stories, presenting them as normative and reinforcing them as the negotiations proceed. Just as Canada is heterogeneous, Tully suggests, so too are people's conceptions of Canada, meaning that "the requirement of unity is an illusion."[33] Despite this acknowledgment, rather than disengage from the Canadian conversation, Tully remains concerned to locate the spaces of agreement or "middle ground," which he does in the criss-crossing and overlapping of the various competing conceptions over time, through the evolving assortment of stories expressed in the Canadian conversation.[34] For Tully, as for the others, the conversation must continue.

The problem with his approach is that it presents the alternative conceptions as if they are simply different understandings that just happen to conflict at various points. Though they may generate sharp recognition struggles when they conflict, they need not conflict if only the participants took more time to understand one another and thus overcome their "diversity blindness." Tully's prescription, then, is to call for greater intercultural understanding. Although this seems reasonable enough, it is difficult to believe that the participants in the Canadian conversation are unaware of the diversity of their alternative conceptions. Far from being "diversity blind," it is more plausible that the differences and especially the perceived hierarchies are all that they can "see," at least politically. (I explore this further in Chapter 8.) Each side is acutely aware of the other, since neither conception has meaning or force except in its opposition. Furthermore, as the Calgary Declaration demonstrates, the strategy of each side is to appropriate as much of the "middle ground" into its position as possible, all the while maintaining the mutually exclusive (hierarchical) relationship between its conception and that of the other side.

As the scholars of the Canadian School like to point out, English Canada's various equality-type discourses are driven by nationalist concerns. While I too am troubled by these nationalist concerns, I am speaking here of a nationalist *debate*. Whether it uses the word nation, political community, culture, group, or identity, and whether it proposes civic nationalism, liberal nationalism, constitutional patriotism, or some other formulation, each side of the debate is preoccupied with achieving some form of unity that, regardless of how open to diversity it may be, leads to a clash of nationalisms and identities. Even though these nationalisms are different in their orientation, it is pointless to try to choose between them, since any one formulation will inevitably feed another; nor does it make sense to seek out the "middle ground," to demonstrate with reasoned arguments how close the two sides really are, since the terrain is so ideologically charged.

The Canadian conversation can be seen as a process of normalization, with civilizing effects. Participants continually disagree over how the Canadian political community is defined, but the disagreement itself suggests that they are taking part in the same conversation. Disagreement presumes agreement on what matters, on what problems require resolution, and on what questions are worth asking. Disagreement suggests agreement on what is worth disagreeing about. In this respect, the participants to the Canadian conversation are united in their opposition.

The Canadian conversation operates on the ideological terrain of multicultural nationalism, a space that manages a wide range of liberal contradictions over justice, equality, and diversity. Multicultural nationalism funnels political contestation over these contradictions into polarizing forms of deliberation over the most appropriate relationship between the political community and its parts. The drive to guard against fragmentation, to ensure unity, amounts at a certain level to a defence of these liberal contradictions, but it cannot dream the antagonisms away.

To return to Bonnie Honig's insight, examined at the beginning of this chapter, since a Canadian home space is never constituted in a final sense, the Canadian conversation remains preoccupied with cohesion and stability.

Participation in the Canadian conversation may involve rejecting the totalizing unity of Rousseau, but it still involves dreams of politics as home. There are alternatives, however. Those pursuing a transformative politics can refuse the invitation to participate in the endless quest for a Canadian home space. In rejecting the unity-driven logic of the Canadian conversation, they will be far better positioned to pursue a "creative politics" instead.[35]

chapter three

Just Nationalism? Individual versus Collective Rights

> The political culture of a country crystallizes around its constitution. Each national culture develops a distinctive interpretation of those constitutional principles that are equally embodied in other republican constitutions – such as popular sovereignty and human rights – in light of its own national history. A "constitutional patriotism" based on these interpretations can take the place originally occupied by nationalism.
> – Jürgen Habermas, "The European Nation-State: On the Past and Future of Sovereignty and Citizenship"

> No matter how violently Quebecers and English Canadians disagree, they do so within political cultures that are remarkably similar. So talking about rights is a way of identifying something all Canadians have in common.
> – Michael Ignatieff, *The Rights Revolution*

> Too often contemporary discussion ... sets up an exhaustive dichotomy between individualism and community ... But like most such terms, individualism and community have a common logic underlying their polarity, which makes it possible for them to define each other negatively. Each entails a denial of difference and a desire to bring multiplicity and heterogeneity into unity, though in opposing ways.
> – Iris Marion Young, *Justice and the Politics of Difference*

As discussed in the last chapter, Canadians have yet to constitute themselves as a "people," except insofar as they continue to try. Certainly, the 1982 Charter of Rights and Freedoms has had profound effects that have reverberated throughout Canadian politics. Michael Ignatieff presents this as the "Rights

Revolution,"[1] and it is difficult to ignore the emergence of a Charter patriotism, especially given the efforts of the federal government not only to cultivate such patriotism but to report on its growth to Canadians. For example, during its celebration of the twentieth anniversary of the Charter in 2002, the government proclaimed high levels of public support for the Charter across the country. Because this support included Quebec, the Charter was deemed a success. Success, here, is a synonym for national unity, although the energy and resources devoted to making and publicizing the case suggest not unity but anxiety surrounding its absence.

The Charter, and patriotic feeling for it, have not taken the "place originally occupied by nationalism" in Canadian politics – at least not in the manner Habermas might desire. Instead, the Charter has always been a site of nationalist contestation.[2] Without Quebec's formal approval, Canada remains without its founding document, and thus without its founding ideas, and so the Canadian conversation continues in pursuit of them. With the (not quite founding) Charter, and its (not quite settled) relationship to the Canadian political community added to the mix, the Canadian conversation enters the terrain of "Rights Talk," as Michael Ignatieff calls it, saying, "The issue of whether group rights should prevail over individual ones, and the larger issue of whether Canada is a single political space or a multiplicity of national spaces, has proved irresolvable."[3]

This idea of a clash between individualistic and collectivist political orientations is one of the most familiar interpretations of Canadian politics and history. Take, as another example, Ramsay Cook's interpretation of a Canadian divide reflecting Rousseauian (i.e., collectivist) ideas in Quebec and Lockean (i.e., individualistic) ideas in English Canada.[4] Similarly, Aboriginal peoples are frequently described as collectivist in contrast to non-Aboriginal peoples.[5] While these individualistic versus collectivist interpretations of Canadian politics and history are often criticized, they remain commonplace. Such interpretations have considerable intuitive appeal, especially in the age of the Charter. It seems obvious that the collectivist demands of Quebec, Aboriginal peoples, women's groups, and ethnic groups necessarily clash with a liberal-individualistic perspective. And so the textbook asks, "Should individual rights take precedence over collective rights?" "Yes"? "No"?[6] Alternatively, can they be reconciled?

These questions generate key sites of polarization in the Canadian conversation, evident especially in the work of Charles Taylor. In two widely cited essays, "Shared and Divergent Values" and "The Politics of Recognition," Taylor puts forward what is probably the most influential version of the individual versus collective rights thesis in Canada.[7] Taylor depicts a conflict between individualistic or procedural liberals in English Canada, inspired by the Charter, and communitarian or "substantive" liberals in Quebec.[8] Taylor believes that the two forms of liberalism are incompatible and, as such, Canadians must learn to live alongside one another, despite their divergent worldviews. It is hard not to be drawn into his framing of the Canadian divide, which makes it all the more bewildering: English Canada, the Charter, and English Canada's embrace of the Charter are hardly reflective of liberal individualism as depicted by Taylor, as I will discuss. In order to reconcile the solitudes, Taylor must first construct them and, in particular, the divide between them.

It is not the Charter's liberalism that is problematic to Quebec, but rather its nationalism. Quebec must reject the Charter not because it is against the liberal principles of the Charter, but because it is *for* them. The dilemma for Quebec is how to embrace the principles of the Charter without embracing the Charter. The problem with the Charter is not that that it fails to accommodate both individual and collective rights, but rather that it succeeds in accommodating both so well.

Individualism versus Collectivism

To contextualize the individualism versus collectivism thesis, it is useful to begin with another influential understanding of the historical origins of Canadian political culture: Gad Horowitz's adaptation of Louis Hartz's fragment thesis.[9] Horowitz believes that the key fragment in Canadian political culture is liberalism, but he seeks to explain the presence of a socialist fragment in Canada, since no equivalent fragment exists in the United States. Horowitz argues that the roots of Canadian socialism are in the Tory fragment brought to Canada by the Loyalists. His well-known idea of the "tory touch" is based on the premise that Toryism always had the potential to develop into socialism, since both ideologies are organic in character, in contrast to the individualistic roots of liberalism.

Many Canadian scholars have debated and criticized the Hartz/Horowitz thesis.[10] Janet Ajzenstat and Peter Smith argue that there has never been a significant Tory fragment in Canada. In direct opposition to the Hartz/Horowitz thesis, they depict a divide between liberalism and forms of civic republicanism or communitarianism. Furthermore, they believe that the liberal/civic republican divide has deep historical roots. They maintain that, in various guises, it has been the fundamental division in Canadian politics since the nineteenth century, and is the historical precursor to the contemporary conflict between individualists and collectivists.[11] According to Ajzenstat and Smith, "It is time to reject the notion, so often reiterated in Canadian text books, and so well entrenched in Canadians' hearts, that the political thought of the modern era is marked by a conservative-liberal-socialist progression.

Rather the political thought of the [Canadian] modern period moves between two poles, one reflecting the liberal philosophy of Enlightenment thinkers like John Locke and his successors, and the other the argument of thinkers like Jean-Jacques Rousseau, who rejected the Enlightenment's central tenets."[12]

I shall leave aside the question of whether Ajzenstat and Smith's thesis is in fact more historically accurate than the Hartz/Horowitz thesis. More intriguing is the manner in which these two theses converge. However they define it, and whatever they believe to be its historical roots (i.e., tory, socialist, communitarian, civic republican, etc.), both depict some form of collectivist ideology engaged in conflict with an individualistic liberalism. While so much debate has revolved around the historical roots and character of the ideological position doing battle with liberalism, far less attention has been paid to the characteristics of the liberalism itself. Charles Taylor is an exception,[13] although his depiction merely reinforces the idea of an individualistic/collectivist divide. Perhaps the liberalism, at least in its contemporary variations, is less individualistic and, indeed, more organic than his understanding suggests? To explore this question, I turn now to Taylor's version of this divide.

Taylor's Procedural versus Communitarian Liberalism

In his essay "The Politics of Recognition," Taylor depicts an opposition between procedural and communitarian liberalism as reflective of a deeper and broader historical divide between equal and differentiated citizenship. He characterizes this divide as follows: "For one, the principle of equal respect requires that we treat people in a difference-blind fashion ... For the other, we have to recognize and even foster particularity. The reproach the first makes to the second is just that it violates the principle of nondiscrimination. The reproach the second makes to the first is that it negates identity by forcing people into a homogeneous mold that is untrue to them."[14] Taylor argues that this divide has a deep and complex history, since both positions are rooted in what he calls a "politics of equal recognition" that emerged from the philosophical inquiries of Rousseau, Hegel, and Herder, among others. Paradoxically, the difference position itself stems from the equality position.

Taylor draws on this philosophical lineage to depict the equality and difference discourses in the terms of procedural liberalism versus communitarian liberalism. He points out that with the contemporary politics of difference there is a familiar charge that the equal or same treatment of everyone inevitably amounts to discrimination against certain disadvantaged groups, whether on the basis of gender, race, or other criteria. In order to reach a situation of nondiscrimination and equal respect for all, it is necessary to acknowledge various citizenship-based distinctions and pursue certain kinds of differential treatment.[15] This differentiation sometimes takes a weak form, such as with affirmative action, where the eventual goal is to reach a point where equal treatment can prevail without differentiation. But it also takes a stronger form, as in the case of Quebec, where cultural survival is itself the main goal.

Taylor examines three versions of the politics of equal recognition to determine whether they are guilty of homogenizing difference: the Rousseauian, the neo-Kantian (or procedural liberal), and his own proposal for communitarian liberalism. He interprets Rousseau as driven by the premise that our dependence on others, as in the realm of opinion, leads to a condition of slavery. Where hierarchy exists, invidious comparison is inevitable and thus we are all enslaved. Rousseau's solution, freedom through equality, means that although we will continue to crave the honour and esteem given by others, and in this sense continue to depend on others, this dependence will be equal. For Taylor, this equality and reciprocity "takes the sting out of our dependence on opinion, and makes it compatible with liberty," but it also requires a tight unity of purpose, which "makes possible the equality of esteem, but the fact that esteem is in principle equal in this system is essential to this unity of purpose itself."[16] Rousseau's insistence on a tight unity of purpose requires a rejection of differentiation altogether and is thus likely to be homogenizing.[17] There are, of course, other interpretations of Rousseau. Most interesting, however, is that in turning to the Canadian manifestation of the equal citizenship discourse, Taylor puts Rousseau aside altogether in favour of a neo-Kantian interpretation.

In "Shared and Divergent Values," Taylor is concerned with understanding and reconciling Quebec's and English Canada's conflicting answers to the question, What is Canada for? He notes that, paradoxically, their answers to this existential question increasingly diverge as their values become more similar. For English Canadians, Canada provides law and order, a commitment to collective provisions and regional equalization, bilingualism, multiculturalism, and the Charter of Rights and Freedoms. While the Québécois also value a great deal in this list, Taylor suggests that Canada exists for them primarily as a space in which the Québécois nation can survive and flourish. Taylor depicts this divergence as reflecting the debate that has taken place between Kantian-inspired procedural liberals, such as John Rawls and Ronald Dworkin, and communitarian liberals, such as Taylor himself.[18]

As Taylor presents it, a version of American-style proceduralism has become increasingly dominant in English Canada. This type of liberalism is based on the premise that the state must remain neutral in its relations with its citizens. The state must not endorse, nor should it support, any one person's or group's conception of the good life, since this type of support might discriminate against individuals who wish to pursue an alternative conception of the good. Individual rights and the principle of nondiscrimination (whereby all individuals are treated as equals) are the two pillars of this approach. In contrast, Taylor believes that Quebec's political culture is rooted in a communitarian form of liberalism that is philosophically incompatible with the procedural liberalism of English Canada. The Quebec state must inevitably valorize some ways of living over others – that is, those geared toward preserving or enhancing the French language – thereby contravening the neutral imperative of procedural liberalism.[19] Although bilingualism may appear to have the purpose of protecting the French language throughout Canada, it does not conflict with procedural liberalism because it can be defended in terms of individual rights: all Canadians have equal access to the French and English languages. In contrast, as Taylor says, "The collective goal [of Quebec] goes beyond this. The aim is not only that Francophones be served in French but that there still be Francophones there in the next generation."[20] Taylor wishes to defend this collective goal.

For Taylor, the clash between the two versions of liberalism manifests itself most clearly in English Canada's rejection of the distinct society clause (DSC) for Quebec, which was included in the failed Meech Lake Accord (1987-90).[21] English Canadians view the DSC as having the purpose of providing the government of Quebec with enhanced power and the legitimacy to carry forward its communitarian brand of liberalism. This is not acceptable to English Canadians since their version of procedural liberalism is antithetical to the kind of substantive project of cultural survival that Quebec seeks to pursue.

Taylor sees no philosophical compromise, no middle ground, between the two versions of liberalism. Their fundamental goals cancel each other out. Those who have followed Taylor in viewing the Canadian impasse in terms of procedural and communitarian liberalism have been unable to achieve a resolution, which is not surprising since Taylor himself presents these positions as philosophically incompatible. For example, according to Samuel LaSelva, "The dilemma may simply be irresolvable."[22]

Given this impasse, Taylor argues that procedural liberals in English Canada must simply acknowledge the liberal credentials (i.e., commitment to minority rights) of communitarian liberals in Quebec. If Canadian federalism is to survive, Taylor believes, it must be flexible enough to allow these two versions of liberalism to coexist, and this means that English Canada must refrain from imposing its own version of liberalism on Quebec.

The more serious dilemma for Taylor is that English Canada is increasingly unlikely to make such a concession. As Canadians become more diverse, so will their competing conceptions of the good life, meaning that they will look for unity in liberal proceduralism itself. And Taylor believes that they find unity in the Charter, which explains the rapid emergence of Charter patriotism. Here we come to the crux of Taylor's problematic: "The special status for Quebec is plainly justified on the grounds of the defence and promotion of *la nation canadienne-française* ... But this is a collective goal. The aim is to ensure the flourishing and survival of a community. The new patriotism of the Charter has given an impetus to a philosophy of rights and of non-discrimination that is highly suspicious of collective goals."[23] For Taylor, the clash between English Canada and Quebec occurs because if the Charter's proceduralism is to be the basis for Canadian unity, it must apply to everyone. But the DSC undermines this uniform application since it could mean that the Charter would not apply to the same extent in Quebec. As Taylor puts it, "If the Charter is really serving as common ground, it is hard to accept that its meaning and application may be modulated in one part of the country ... the Charter of all things had to apply in the same way to all Canadians."[24]

Taylor's central argument is that the philosophical divide is not only reflected in the makeup of Canada but widening with the emergence of Charter patriotism. As a result, his own dream of "reconciling the solitudes" appears to be fading away. But perhaps there is another approach. Maybe the reason it is so difficult to reconcile this divide, in the philosophical terms used by Taylor, is that it does not actually exist – except insofar as these terms are used.

Nationalist Justice

It would in fact be surprising if the Charter cultivated proceduralism in English Canada, since it is anything but a straightforward proceduralist or liberal individualist document. While the Charter certainly contains individual rights clauses typical of liberal proceduralism, it also contains others that seem to conflict with procedural liberalism.[25] Indeed, whereas Taylor criticizes the Charter for its proceduralist emphasis, many have celebrated (or disparaged) its mix of individual and collective rights clauses.[26] This suggests that any tension between procedural liberalism and communitarian liberalism is part of the Charter itself; even the Charter's main nondiscrimination or equality clause contains what may be interpreted as a collectivist subclause.[27] The mix of individual and collective rights clauses in the Charter has been characterized by Michael Ignatieff, Simone Chambers, Thomas Berger, and many others as one of its *defining* features and as providing a distinctive alternative to the individualism of the American constitutional model.[28]

Taylor might point out that what is really at issue is that many English Canadians have *embraced* the Charter on proceduralist grounds. If English Canadians perceive the Charter as proceduralist and if they view the DSC as likely to weaken the scope and application of the Charter, then their rejection of the DSC would be proceduralist in character. While he acknowledges that some Charter provisions may give power to collectivities, Taylor argues that the individual rights and equal treatment (or nondiscrimination) principles "dominate in the public consciousness."[29] But do they?

Much of Taylor's case rests on the controversy surrounding Quebec's language laws and, in particular, the Quebec government's use of the notwithstanding clause to shield Bill 178 from the Charter and the Supreme Court. Many members of the English language minority in Quebec, such as those who wanted to advertise their businesses predominantly in English, expressed strong opposition to the DSC on the grounds that it would provide even greater powers to the government of Quebec to employ such measures.[30] As Kenneth McRoberts points out, however, English Canadian opposition to the DSC – and the Meech Lake Accord generally – was strong before the Quebec government's use of the notwithstanding clause.[31] Indeed, more notable here is the *infrequency* with which individual rights-based arguments have been put forward by English Canadians outside of Quebec.[32] As Janet Ajzenstat laments, "The true – and, I would argue, sad – fact about Canada today is that the rest of Canada is not vitally concerned about Quebec's treatment of its citizens, or any other issues relating to that province's internal policies."[33] In English Canada, the anti-DSC equality discourse has not been centrally concerned with the treatment of anglophones *within* Quebec.

Scholars studying this arena offer numerous, and often incompatible, depictions of Charter politics, suggesting that the English Canadian embrace of the Charter is driven by a conflicting assortment of principles and goals.[34] The entrenchment of the Charter has led feminist activists, Aboriginal organizations, ethnic groups, religious groups, gay and lesbian organizations, and others to pursue rights-based strategies for change.[35] While there is much debate about the efficacy of these strategies, they are hardly proceduralist in any straightforward sense, nor are the responses of their critics.[36]

In these ways, Taylor's interpretation seems quite flawed, and others have arrived at much the same conclusion. Thus, Joseph Carens suggests that Taylor "overstates the difference" between the political cultures of Quebec and English Canada.[37] For Guy Laforest, "the 1982 Charter of Rights and Freedoms, as well as the political culture of English-speaking Canada, makes ample room for Taylor's two models of liberalism."[38] Louis Balthazar notes that "Canadians have always understood, through their history and traditions, that individual rights, as primordial and precious as they may be, are empty if they are not complemented by collective rights."[39] Finally, according to Ramsay Cook, "The Charter articulates both a 'rights model' and a 'community model,' though not in the fashion preferred by those who agree with Charles Taylor."⁴⁰ If Taylor's interpretation is so influential despite being so flawed, there must be more to it – notwithstanding all its critics. And there is indeed more to it, partly *because* of all of its critics.

Taylor's argument is intuitively attractive because the equality discourse obviously resembles procedural liberal principles. Consider the familiar complaints of English Canadians who reject the DSC and other forms of differentiation, using language such as "Why are *they* so special?" and "We should all be treated equally." Taylor is quite right to make a strong connection between the equality discourse and unity, yet he gets this connection backward where procedural liberalism is concerned. As he puts it, "Dworkin claims that a liberal society is one which, as a society, adopts no particular substantive view about the ends of life. Rather, the society is *united around* strong procedural commitments to treat people with equal respect."⁴¹ If we accept this premise, it is not surprising that the equality discourse became a basis for unity. But is unity the *result* of the equality strategy, or is unity its main *purpose*?

Procedural liberals such as Rawls and Dworkin might agree that the end result of the principle of nondiscrimination could be cohesion and unity, and they would probably view this unity positively. They would never suggest, however, that unity is the overriding purpose of the procedural liberal application of equal treatment. The purpose of procedural liberalism is to ensure freedom and human dignity, as they understand these concepts. Unity (of certain types) is welcomed, to be sure, but it represents, at best, a derivative good. Key here is the distinction between goal-based (teleological) and rights-based (deontological) theories of justice. Whereas Rawls and Dworkin ground their theories of justice in the latter, the English Canadian equality discourse is driven by the former (the primary goal being national unity). As Rawls explains, in teleological theories, "the good is defined independently from the right, and then the right is defined as that which maximizes the good."⁴²

In contrast to the theorizing of Dworkin and Rawls, the Canadian version of the equal treatment discourse is driven less by principles of liberal justice than by dreams of a single cohesive political community. This is where it might be helpful were Rousseau to reenter Taylor's analysis. Few serious philosophical accounts of procedural equality argue that equality necessarily entails the *same* treatment at all times. For Dworkin, "The right to treatment as an equal is fundamental, and the right to equal treatment, derivative. In some circumstances the right to treatment as an equal will entail a right to equal treatment, but not, by any means, in all circumstances."⁴³ This means that, sometimes, treating people as equals will mean treating them differently in certain respects. Yet in the Canadian case, the dogmatic insistence upon uniformity in the application of the Charter betrays the equal citizenship discourse, demonstrating that it is primarily interested in using equality to ensure unity as opposed to using equality in order to pursue liberal principles of justice. Only because the Charter has the purpose of unity must it be applied in a uniform manner to all Canadians.

Reconstituting the Solitudes

Of course, Taylor knows all of this – perhaps as well as anyone.[44] He is disturbed by the nationalism of English Canada and its embrace of the Charter. Still, the Charter is a site of nationalist contestation through and through. Its nationalism is immune to reasoned deliberation. But Taylor's procedural liberal versus communitarian liberal framing cannot be dismissed as simply fictional. One of the characteristics of the Canadian conversation is that it frames nationalist contestation in abstract, often philosophical, terms. Taylor's interpretation distorts matters, but this is precisely the point. Taylor is doing far more than interpreting the Canadian conversation; he is participating in it – shaping it. Because of its influence, Taylor's framing of the Quebec/English Canadian relationship is "real."

By framing this contestation in the philosophical terms of procedural liberalism versus communitarian liberalism, Taylor gives each side of the debate internal coherence, while providing clarity to the difference between them. Of course, the worldviews of Canadians, whether in English Canada or in Quebec, are unlikely to be as philosophically coherent as Taylor's depiction suggests. But the depiction itself – and the debate it is part of – serves to construct them as if they were philosophically coherent. Taylor constructs the two sides as if each were unified by the difference between them.[45]

Why is Taylor so invested in marking the difference between the "solitudes"? The problem for Québécois nationalists is less the content of the Charter and more the nationalism inherent within it, as an instrument of pan-Canadian unity. Quebec must reject the Charter not because it is against Charter principles, but despite the fact that it is for them. The Charter is problematic not because it is so individualistic, but because it is not – that is, because the Charter *can* accommodate Quebec's collectivist concerns. The dilemma, for Quebec nationalists, is that their necessary non-embrace of the Charter is easily depicted by their pan-Canadian opponents as illustrating illiberalism. After all, why else would they reject the Charter unless they were sliding down the slippery slope toward ethnic nationalism?

This framing is obviously anathema to contemporary Quebec nationalists. Still, the charge of ethnic nationalism forces the minority nationalism on the defensive. The trick is to put its liberal values forward while continuing to emphasize its difference from English Canada's Charter. Taylor does this by reframing the divide in procedural liberal/communitarian liberal terms, replacing the common civic/ethnic framing. Quebec is liberal, but liberal in a different way. To construct Quebec as distinct, but still liberal, Taylor paints a liberal individualistic picture of English Canada, without which there would be nothing to differentiate Quebec's liberalism from.

The Canadian conversation constructs and reinforces the axis of difference between the "solitudes," and, in doing so, orients them to one another along *liberal* terms. The debate civilizes both Québécois and pan-Canadian nationalisms to a liberal terrain, even while reinforcing the national difference. Put in another way, there is not much difference between Quebec and English Canada when considered in terms of liberal principles, but the continuation of a debate necessarily constructs and reinforces a difference.

According to Michael Ignatieff, Beverley McLachlin, and many others, the Charter does not put an end to all debate; it is, rather, an important forum for discussion.[46] But what is the nature of the discussion? Where questions of individual and collective rights are concerned, the discussion is less about justice than about nationalist contestation framed in terms of justice.

chapter four

Decoding Deep Diversity

> The people of Quebec must also understand the rest of the country has a soul too.
> – Premier Clyde Wells, testimony to Beaudoin-Dobbie Committee, 1992

> What a stroke of inspiration. Quebecers are unique. We could be tempted to add: "Like everybody else!"
> – Lucien Bouchard, to the media, 17 September 1997

> Canadian constitutional culture is not ideological.
> – James Tully, "Diversity's Gambit Declined," 1992

In this chapter, I arrive at what may be called the heavyweight category of Canadian nationalist contestation: the recognition or lack thereof of Quebec as nation and a distinct society within the Canadian federation. This issue has been the central concern of Canada's unity debates for decades, and it has preoccupied the political and intellectual classes throughout Canada's history. Recently, especially with the Charter, so-called average citizens have begun jumping into the ring. And no wonder. In its sharpest form – equal provinces or asymmetrical federalism? – it is a proxy for the national question itself.

Anyone exploring this terrain, which seems increasingly immune to originality, cannot help but worry that anything said will merely serve to reproduce old patterns. This is no less so when one wishes, as I do, to study the patterns themselves. It is fitting, then, to continue my examination of Charles Taylor's work, since few have studied the patterns with greater clarity or reproduced them with more originality.

Taylor's notion of "deep diversity" is one of the most widely discussed and appropriated concepts in contemporary Canadian scholarship.[1] Taylor presents deep diversity as a means of reconciling Quebec's demands for recognition and greater autonomy on the one hand, and the Western provinces' demands for increased power at the federal level on the other hand. By supplementing the shallower diversity of the Canadian mosaic, and by accommodating asymmetrical patterns of belonging in Canada, deep diversity creates spaces of recognition for a Québécois nation and Aboriginal peoples within the Canadian political community. As such, it seems to have the potential to resolve Canada's perpetual problem of national unity. With deep diversity, everybody seems to win – but is it all too good to be true?

To find out, I place Taylor's deep diversity concept in its historical context: Canadian constitutional negotiations. This chapter begins by examining the logic of the Meech Lake constitutional process (1987-90), which Taylor's concept responded to, and the subsequent Charlottetown process (1992). I then analyze the Calgary Declaration (1997), which took the equal provinces versus asymmetrical federalism divide to a new extreme by rejecting the notion of Quebec as a distinct society in favour of viewing all of the provinces as equally unique. These opposing ideas – equal uniqueness and deep diversity – each recognize one understanding of the Canadian political community while necessarily misrecognizing the other understanding. In the concluding section, I argue that deep diversity, instead of displacing the opposition between provincial equality and asymmetrical federalism, sharpens its polarizing logic in static identitarian terms.

The Meech Lake Formula

The scholarship on the Meech Lake Accord is abundant, as is work on Canadian constitutional politics in general.[2] I shall assume that the main outlines of the case are familiar to anyone with any knowledge of contemporary Canadian politics – especially since it continues to have a large influence. Instead of describing it in any detail, I shall simply outline its basic logic.

The Accord was known as the "Quebec Round" because it was designed to meet the five minimum conditions put forward by the Liberal government of Quebec for Quebec's signing the Constitution Act, 1982.[3] Despite the great complexity of Canadian constitutional politics, the formula for the agreement among the first ministers at Meech Lake remains deceptive in its simplicity: keep it symmetrical, at least in principle, by giving Quebec the powers it demands and by providing all the other provinces with access to all these powers as well.[4] The reason for the Accord's eventual failure was equally deceptive in its simplicity: Quebec's demand to be recognized as distinct could not, like all the other demands, be distributed symmetrically. The distinct society principle and the symmetry principle do not simply clash – each is designed to annul the other. There is no grey space between them, although recent constitutional negotiations have attempted to find some. David Milne points out, "Any realistic look at the Meech Lake Accord itself would surely show that, with the single exception of the 'distinct society' clause, the equality principle trumped on every element of the package in the so-called Quebec round. Despite the fact that Quebec had tabled proposals providing for asymmetry over the veto in the amending formula and some other subjects, first ministers reasserted equality at every turn."[5]

Even though it was surrounded by equality-based provisions emphasizing symmetry, the distinct society clause generated intense hostility, especially outside of Quebec. So strong was the opposition that in the period leading up to the Accord's eventual failure in 1990, the first ministers made frantic attempts to dilute the distinct society clause further through amendments to the original agreement.[6]

The failure of Meech has had effects far beyond the constitutional arena, not the least of which was to propel the Canadian federal party system into a period of realignment. Prior to Meech, all three major federal parties were united in favouring the recognition of Quebec as distinct, leaving the fledgling Reform Party alone to harness the "no special treatment for Quebec" resentment of many English Canadians. Meanwhile, English Canada's rejection of recognizing Quebec as distinct reinvigorated separatist feelings in Quebec and created a space for them in Ottawa too, with the formation of the Bloc Québécois one month after the fall of Meech.

Taylor's Deep Diversity
Following the failure of Meech, Charles Taylor proposed his idea of deep diversity. Taylor depicts the constitutional impasse as revolving around a conflict between, on the one hand, the demand for greater autonomy for Quebec via a distinct society clause and, on the other hand, more power for certain English Canadian regions and provinces at the federal level in Ottawa. Taylor argues that these two demands are institutionally compatible and that this is, in effect, not a real tension at all. According to Taylor, "One side [i.e., Quebec] wants to take a greater distance from the central government and legislature. The other [especially Western Canadians] wants a weightier place within them." He argues that "these demands are not logically opposed."[7] Asymmetrical federalism can provide Quebec with more autonomy, and this can easily coexist with a reformed Senate, thereby providing the Western provinces with more power at the federal level in Ottawa. These two changes are

constitutionally and institutionally compatible because, Taylor argues, "special status (for Quebec) has nothing to do with having more clout at the centre."[8]

Instead, deep diversity means that different groups of people – whether provinces, Aboriginal peoples, or ethnic groups – may develop their attachment to the Canadian political community in different ways. Taylor presents this idea as follows:

> To build a country for everyone, Canada would have to allow for second-level or "deep" diversity, in which a plurality of ways of belonging would also be acknowledged and accepted. Someone of, say, Italian extraction in Toronto or Ukrainian extraction in Edmonton might indeed feel Canadian as a bearer of individual rights in a multicultural mosaic. His or her belonging would not "pass through" some other community, although the ethnic identity might be important to him or her in various ways. But this person might nevertheless accept that a Québécois or a Cree or a Déné might belong in a very different way, that these persons were Canadian through being members of their national communities. Reciprocally, the Québécois, Cree, or Déné would accept the perfect legitimacy of the "mosaic" identity.[9]

As Taylor would have it, a framework of deep diversity does not mean that some groups are privileged over others; all individuals and groups are of equal value. Because their relationships to the larger political community may vary, however, there must be a mechanism flexible enough to accommodate these variations.

Everyone can belong to the Canadian political community as they like; for Québécois and Aboriginal people, their collective memberships can be given greater recognition, with their membership in the Canadian political community recognized as secondary. For all others, their regional, provincial, ethnic, religious or cultural diversity can be recognized too, although in a shallower manner, while providing greater recognition to their sense of belonging to the Canadian political community as a whole. In Taylor's framing, everyone appears to get what they want. Still, instead of reconciling the opposition, deep diversity only heightens it further, as I will illustrate.

Taylor's argument emerged out of a particular moment in Canadian constitutional history. Still, the logic of his analysis has relevance beyond the Meech Lake Accord, since the terms of the debate have not changed very much. Indeed, they only became sharper with the Charlottetown Accord and the Calgary Declaration.

A Symmetry at Charlottetown

The Charlottetown Accord was a far more wide-ranging document that attempted to deal with many of the criticisms made by English Canadians, Aboriginal peoples, and minorities of the Meech Lake Accord. The strategy of the first ministers was, in effect, to include a distinct society clause for Quebec but to surround it with even more equality provisions, so as to ensure that only a minimal degree of symbolic asymmetry resulted. Most of the relevant provisions were included up front in a "Canada clause," which outlined the "fundamental characteristics" of Canada. The third provision of the Canada clause states, "Quebec constitutes within Canada a distinct society, which includes a French-speaking majority, a unique culture and a civil law tradition."[10] This provision is balanced and contained by the eighth provision of the Canada clause, which reads, "Canadians confirm the principle of the equality of the provinces at the same time as recognizing their diverse characteristics."[11] Following this is a second distinct society clause that states, "The role of the legislature and Government of Quebec to preserve and promote the distinct society of Quebec is affirmed."[12] Potential asymmetry resulting from the two distinct society clauses is then limited by a further provision that appears toward the end of the Charlottetown text, stating that any agreement between the federal government and one province must be available to all the other provinces in order to "accord that other government equality of treatment."[13] Thus while Quebec is recognized as a distinct society, this recognition is set firmly within an equal provinces framework.

During the referendum campaign, many Canadians rejected even this diluted and contained distinct society clause. More than anyone, Pierre Trudeau cultivated this rejection in his famous "Maison Egg-Roll" speech, in which he interpreted the equal provinces provision thus: "That's really something: they confirm the equality of the provinces, after having said in the same article, in a sub-clause, that Quebec is a *distinct* society and it is the *only* distinct province in the Constitution. So what is this now about telling the provinces they are all equal?"[14]

The opposing positions clashed throughout the referendum campaign, such as in the following television exchange between Jim Nielsen, a BC politician, and then federal justice minister Kim Campbell:

> *Nielsen:* I think it would be dreadfully wrong for the country to introduce a system whereby the provinces and the people of the country are not to be treated equally ...
>
> *Campbell:* But they've never been treated equally ... The whole, the whole principle of Canadian confederation ... is that we treat

people differently to ensure that they can be equal. And that is the great fallacy in this debate, that somehow equality is sameness. It's not sameness.

Nielsen: Of course it's not sameness, it's ...

Campbell: If you treat me the way you are treated, as a woman ... the result will be that I will be unequal in many, many circumstances.

Nielsen: No, I appreciate that, but we have to be practical too. We can't obviously give someone a distinct advantage. We and other parts of the country are distinct too.[15]

A distinction, it seems, is a distinction, no matter how much symmetry surrounds it. This polarizing pattern of deliberation was a defining feature of the Charlottetown referendum campaign, which illustrates further my critique of the new constitutionalism thesis discussed in Chapter 2.

Brubaker's Architectonic Illusion

Canadian constitutional politics reflects what Rogers Brubaker calls the "architectonic illusion"[16] – the illusion that nationalist contestation may be "solved" through the construction of the "right" constitutional or institutional framework.[17] This illusion propels the Canadian conversation forward. The deliberative process achieves agreement on so many issues that an overarching consensus has often seemed close. This is because much of the Canadian conversation is taken up with the following areas of convergence, even though they are, at the end of the day, not what it is *really* about:

Division of powers As both the Meech Lake and Charlottetown Accords demonstrated, this is an area characterized by significant agreement in recent constitutional rounds. Whatever powers Quebec gets, the other provinces may assume as well.

Decentralization Some people worry that if Quebec assumes greater powers, other provinces will do the same, leading toward greater decentralization of the federation. Brian Schwartz calls this "buffet federalism."[18] Putting aside whether Canadians should be concerned about decentralization, it is an important area of convergence between the positions of Quebec and the West. Although Taylor presents deep diversity as an institutional solution to these two issues – the division of powers and decentralization – both are areas of convergence in the Canadian conversation.

Democratic legitimacy When a province assumes power in a given policy area, does this mean that federal MPs from that province should not be able to play a federal role in that policy area? While such questions of democratic legitimacy and accountability are real, they have never been serious obstacles to agreement.[19]

Conflicting liberal and communitarian political cultures Contra Taylor, English Canadian proponents of equal provinces have expressed little concern over providing Quebec with powers to preserve and develop its distinctive culture; instead, they want access to these powers for their own provinces too.

These sorts of issues will undoubtedly preoccupy scholars of federalism, constitutional lawyers, and federal-provincial bureaucrats. Still, while they provide plenty of topics for the Canadian conversation, they are of secondary importance to it. The Canadian conversation requires not just agreement on institutional design but also an understanding of what such agreement means for the constitution of the political community. What matters is not the way Canada actually operates, or the way federalism is practised, but the way it is understood. As a result, while deliberation takes place, and agreement on many issues is reached, it all disintegrates rather quickly. And when it does, the national question is blamed, as if it had somehow got in the way at the last minute, whether by accident, bad luck, or ill will on the part of one's negotiating partners.

In the same way, deep diversity succeeds splendidly in areas of agreement, but it fails where Taylor most wants it to succeed: on the national question. This is where (and why) the Canadian conversation congeals into its polarized form. Consider Taylor's language: "The task [of resolving the impasse] will be utterly impossible if we persist in describing the problem in the misleading and often demagogic language of equality versus inequality of provinces. Put in these terms, *the problem is a false one,* and the present importance of this formulation is a sign of our lack of lucidity and the decline of good will."[20] Maybe deep diversity really is too good to be true, for when Taylor finally comes to the problem, he declares it "false." Solutions like deep diversity are enticing because they reframe the problem itself, as if doing so will make it (and one's opponents) disappear. This reframing enables the conclusion that the solution works fine; it is the problem that is problematic. Taylor, like everyone who takes part in the Canadian conversation, can deliberate productively on virtually every matter of concern, except the real (false?) matter of concern.

The equal provinces discourse is coated in resentment, to be sure, but this makes it no less real.[21] Pretending otherwise only reinforces the antagonism.

We have reason to expect from Taylor a better understanding of the nationalist desire for recognition and community underpinning this resentment. The equal provinces discourse is hardly anticommunitarian. Instead, it is a rejection of the idea that Quebec should be allowed a *greater* ability to preserve its culture than others. And it is an insistence that the Canadian political community be defined by the equal recognition of such *collective* projects. This is not procedural liberalism, but more like a procedural communitarianism; it is not a clash with communitarianism, but a communitarian clash. To illustrate, I turn to the Calgary Declaration.

The Calgary Declaration: Equally Unique
The Calgary Declaration was negotiated in 1997 by all the provincial premiers and territorial leaders, except Premier Bouchard of Quebec. The prime minister was not present, and nor were Aboriginal leaders. The negotiations centred on two competing requirements, which remained much the same as in earlier constitutional rounds. The urgency surrounding the first one – providing recognition to Quebec – was clear, given the narrow victory of the federalists in the 1995 Quebec referendum. Yet the premiers were also preoccupied by the second – the equality of the provinces and of Canadian citizens generally. This second requirement is evident in the wording of the Calgary Declaration itself:

1. All Canadians are equal and have rights protected by law.
2. All provinces, while diverse in their characteristics, have equality of status.
3. Canada is graced by a diversity, tolerance, compassion and an equality of opportunity that is without rival in the world.
4. Canada's gift of diversity includes Aboriginal peoples and cultures, the vitality of the English and French languages and a multicultural citizenry drawn from all parts of the world.
5. In Canada's federal system, where respect for diversity and equality underlies unity, the unique character of Quebec society, including its French speaking majority, its culture and its tradition of civil law, is fundamental to the well being of Canada. Consequently, the legislature and Government of Quebec have a role to protect and develop the unique character of Quebec society within Canada.
6. If any future constitutional amendment confers powers on one province, these powers must be available to all provinces.
7. Canada is a federal system where federal, provincial, and territorial governments work in partnership while respecting

each other's jurisdictions. Canadians want their governments to work cooperatively and with flexibility to ensure the efficiency and effectiveness of the federation. Canadians want their governments to work together particularly in the delivery of their social programs. Provinces and territories renew their commitment to work in partnership with the Government of Canada to best serve the needs of Canadians.[22]

The sticking point in the Calgary negotiations was the form and relationship between what later became clauses 5 and 6. The phrase "unique character of Quebec society" was proposed as an alternative to the phrase "distinct society," which carried so much baggage from the Meech Lake and Charlottetown rounds. Driven by Premiers Glen Clark of British Columbia and Ralph Klein of Alberta, most of the negotiations centred on how to ensure that this statement as well as the accompanying phrase "the legislature and Government of Quebec have a role to protect and develop the unique character of Quebec society within Canada" would be channelled and contained. The key for these premiers was to make sure that clause 5 did not confer, or appear to confer, "special treatment" upon Quebec. There was considerable disagreement as to whether a qualifying statement should be part of clause 5, or should make up its own clause 6.[23] According to one journalistic account, the third draft of the declaration, proposed by the "hard-line" premiers, included the following: "It is not the intention of this proposal to confer additional powers, but if any powers are conferred on one province as a result of this proposal, then these powers should apply equally to any other province in comparable circumstances."[24] This statement was seen as too confrontational by several of the premiers and a compromise, brokered by Premier Mike Harris of Ontario, led Premiers Clark and Klein to adopt a less aggressive posture toward Quebec. Eventually, the statement was rewritten as clause 6. The recognition of Quebec's uniqueness was thus situated firmly within the confines of provincial equality.

In all of this, the premiers were very attuned to the equal-citizenship parameters set forth by the Reform Party, which had just become the Official Opposition.[25] As Rosemary Speirs of the *Toronto Star* put it, "The provincial leaders tried to find a formula so innocuous even a Manning couldn't object."[26] According to *Maclean's*, "Fearful of starting what one premier called 'a political grassfire in the West,' the nine [premiers] made sure the document would be acceptable to Reform party Leader Preston Manning, who is so in tune with hard-line opinion towards Quebec separatists. They even chose to use many of Manning's own words ... As the premiers prepared to leave Calgary's stately McDougall Centre to tell the country of their accomplishment, Ontario Premier Mike Harris phoned Manning to tell him: 'You won.'"[27]

In placing the Calgary Declaration before their provincial constituents, the premiers attempted to preempt claims of "special treatment" at every opportunity.[28] They emphasized that the declaration was designed to allow Quebec space to preserve its "uniqueness" without providing it with anything beyond what other provinces may also receive. The website of the Saskatchewan government illustrated this framing well, posing for itself the dreaded but expected question, "Aren't the Premiers just coming back at us with another special deal for Quebec?" Its response: "The answer is NO. This isn't a special deal for any one province ... People in Quebec who believe in Canada need to hear the rest of us say that they can be in Canada and protect their language, culture and legal system – that's principle 5 ... The rest of us need to hear that there will be no special deals for any one province ... that's principle 6."[29] Yet despite all of their efforts, the premiers faced a skeptical public, as illustrated in the following radio exchange between Newfoundland premier Brian Tobin and an unidentified telephone caller:

> *Caller:* I really don't agree with the statement because I think you're actually appeasing Quebec people again by the inclusion of the word "unique" ... I mean it's really – you know – that seems to be quite clear to everybody. Now I must say I don't have any allegiance to any particular party, but I do pick out the issues that I like and one of the things at the last election – I appreciated Preston Manning's statement – that he thought all Canadians should be treated equally.
>
> *Tobin:* But, you know, Preston Manning supports the Calgary Declaration ... the first words of the statement, the Calgary Declaration, are: "All Canadians are equal."
>
> *Caller:* Yes – but by asserting the word "unique," it sort of – it cancels that out.
>
> *Tobin:* ... I think we've got to bear in mind that these are premiers from provinces that are certainly not in the business of appeasing Quebec: British Columbia and Alberta and so on.[30]

The language here is telling. According to the *Concise Oxford Dictionary*, the word "appease" means "make calm or quiet, esp. conciliate (a potential aggressor) by making concessions ... satisfy (an appetite, scruples)."[31]

The Calgary Declaration deals with diversity by tethering it to a layer of equal treatment. The words "equality" or "equal" appear in clauses 1, 2, 3, and 5, and are implied in clause 6. The words "diversity" or "diverse" appear in clauses 2, 3, 4, and 5. "Diversity" is used to describe the uniqueness of *each* of the provinces and of Aboriginal peoples and ethnic groups. "Equality" is used to make it clear that these manifestations of diversity are to be appropriately contained by equal treatment. Just as the citizens are diverse *but* equal, so too are the provinces: all the provinces must have a uniform degree of leeway in charting their relationship with Canada as a whole. Quebec can do much to preserve its "unique character," but nothing that other provinces cannot also do.

Not surprisingly, the premiers emphasized to their constituents their use of the phrase "unique character," while rejecting the phrase "distinct society." For example, the government of Saskatchewan asked itself the question, "Why should the [Calgary Declaration] refer specifically to Quebec's unique character?" Its answer: "In a sense, there is nothing unique about Quebec's uniqueness. Nor is there anything unique about the Quebec government's responsibilities toward its uniqueness. Nevertheless, this Principle is in accord with Canada's oldest constitutional traditions ... This practice reflects the particular sense of vulnerability felt by North America's only French-speaking jurisdiction to being assimilated and, thereby, to being eradicated as a society with a unique character." It then goes on to say, "Naturally, it is not only Quebec that has unique characteristics. The *same claim* can be made for all the provinces and territories of Canada."[32]

Similarly, according to the Newfoundland government's website, "'distinct' suggests a 'separateness' that is *inconsistent with the concept of unity*. By contrast, 'unique character' suggests something special that does not undermine unity, and therefore more accurately describes what is meant."[33] The distinction between "distinct" and "unique" received considerable attention.[34] Of course, the shift is largely a matter of symbolic baggage, since "distinct" had come to mean "special treatment" for Quebec. What is interesting is that since the term "unique" could easily take on much the same connotation, it is tied down heavily by the frequent usage of the term "equality." "Equality" has the effect of suppressing the symbolic force that the word "unique" would otherwise have. Consider, for example, the way Preston Manning framed his support for the Calgary Declaration, endorsing the premiers' use of the phrase "unique character" because "they linked the acknowledgment of uniqueness to the principles of equality of citizens and provinces." He went on to warn that some would try to turn this back into a "modified distinct society clause by decoupling it from the equality principle."[35] Whatever word is used – "distinct" or "unique" – the difference of Quebec is limited by the layer of symmetry tied to equality. Quebec is different, but no different in its difference.

Quebec is effectively put in its place as just one of ten unique provinces (rather than one of two or more nations), making it possible for Stéphane Dion, the federal "unity" minister, to say, "The premiers have destroyed the 'special status' argument."[36] Similarly, according to Prime Minister Jean Chrétien, the Calgary Declaration "makes it clear that citizens are equal in Canada, provinces are equal in Canada, but there is diversity in our society that has been the trademark of Canada, this ability to have diversity but unity at the same time."[37]

As much as Chrétien attempts to suggest otherwise, this "diversity but unity" approach does not resolve matters, as shown by the many hostile reactions to the Calgary Declaration. For example, Premier Lucien Bouchard of Quebec responded, "But we are unique, they say, by the language of our majority, by our culture and our civil-code tradition ... So what? What will it give us? What will it change? Nothing! What a stroke of inspiration. Quebecers are unique. We could be tempted to add: 'Like everyone else!' ... 'Unique' like the SkyDome, Cape Breton, Labatt Blue or Wayne Gretzky. This expression would render us both socially unique and a political eunuch."[38] Elsewhere, Bouchard called the Calgary Declaration "a trap ... an attempt to make Quebec's national reality disappear ... the more we examine it, the more we see that our Canadian neighbours' text belittles us, holds us back, reduces us."[39] These comments are as we would expect; Bouchard rejected the equality discourse as a discourse of containment, emphasizing Quebec difference instead.

Phil Fontaine, national chief of the Assembly of First Nations, rejected the Calgary Declaration on similar grounds: "We accept, with generosity and kindness, multicultural groups and visible minorities ... But we are different – we are as well unique." In other words, Aboriginal peoples cannot be constrained within the symmetrical notion of diversity implied by multiculturalism. The article containing this statement notes that Fontaine "criticized the declaration for promoting equality of all citizens and blamed the Reform party for making it the norm in Canadian politics. 'It's an attempt to deny the fact that we were here first, that we are unique, that we have our own languages, our own traditions, our own values, our own history.'"[40] For Fontaine, equal treatment is an attempt to suppress difference, a move that he resists by reasserting the differences of Aboriginal peoples.

In this way, each term of the equal provinces versus asymmetrical federalism opposition presupposes and nourishes the other. The recognition of Quebec as distinct creates a symbolic asymmetry that amounts to a denial of English Canada's own symmetrical view of the Canadian community.

English Canadians in turn attempt to reassert symbolic symmetry by insisting that all of the provinces must be equal. There is no problem, they insist, with Quebec having increased powers to preserve and develop its unique culture; indeed, this is Quebec's responsibility. Yet this responsibility cannot be *distinct*, since it applies to other Canadian communities as well. This approach necessarily fails to accommodate Quebec's distinct recognition demand, producing an endless recognition struggle wherein the terms in opposition reverse continually.

The two sets of collective recognition demands clash because the basis of community upon which each pursues recognition is antithetical to the other. Importantly, this is not some unfortunate coincidence: the two sets of demands do not simply happen to conflict. Rather, the recognition demands presuppose one another as mutually exclusive. Yet this is not a zero-sum game, since there is no stable sum of recognition to struggle over; the recognition demands have no meaning outside of the opposition. Each demand gains in importance as it is denied. As this manifestation of the Canadian conversation continues, the struggle between the nationalisms is sharpened, with their competing identities put forward in increasingly totalizing terms. This is the site of the impasse, which no amount of institutional manoeuvring can possibly solve.

Rousseauian Dreams of Clarity

Given the Calgary Declaration, how can we attain a better understanding of the equal citizens and provinces discourse? Taylor emphasizes the value of Canada as a place where Quebec's recognition needs may be met. However, he is less concerned with demands for group or collective recognition emanating from within English Canada. This may be because of his mistaken assumption that, whereas nationalists in Quebec (and Aboriginal peoples) are communitarian, English Canadians are liberal-individualists whose sense of self is not tied to forms of collective recognition. But when we examine the English Canadian answer to Taylor's question "Why Canada?" we begin to see the extent to which the equality discourse is also a type of recognition claim. For English Canadians, Canada is the political community within which all citizens are given an equal opportunity to develop their own sense of national belonging – and are recognized for this equal opportunity. Such recognition appears to be the essence of deep diversity.

Taylor might very well respond that what he is objecting to is the insistence upon *provincial* equality, which need not have any direct connection to the equal recognition of individual Canadians. Since the layering of Canadian citizenship is shaped by federalism, however, it should not be surprising that the English Canadian demand for equal recognition flows into a demand for provincial equality. In order to ensure equal respect for all Canadians, as citizens of provincially based communities, each province must have an equal ability to chart its own course within the federation. As soon as one province or community is labelled distinct, it is viewed as having achieved a privileged status: not just different, but recognized as different.

The Calgary Declaration's equality discourse operates within the terms of what Michel Foucault calls the Rousseauian dream of "a transparent society, visible and legible in each of its parts, the dream of there no longer existing any zones of darkness, zones established by the privileges of royal power or the prerogatives of some corporation, zones of disorder."[41] This discourse is driven by a need for simplicity and clarity, so that everyone (and every group) understands how they relate to others in the context of the whole. Deep diversity – precisely because of its "depth" – seems to provide an alternative to English Canada's Rousseauian dreams. The longing for unity, identity, and clarity, however, is common to *both* sides of the debate.

The symmetrical framework sets up a hierarchy of belonging, recognizing pan-Canadian differences over Québécois difference. In response, Taylor argues that the Québécois and Aboriginal peoples are entitled to a nationalist or communitarian space within Canada. At first glance, deep diversity seems to allow any grouping of citizens to develop alternative forms of belonging to the broader political community. But the recognition of a "deeper" form of diversity for some is meaningful only if it is distinct, which means that it must be exclusive. Taylor's task, with deep diversity, is to clarify the character of the asymmetry by delineating precisely which groups are to be recognized as relating to the Canadian political community in a "deeply" differentiated manner. The recognition of layered belonging is limited to Quebec and the Aboriginal peoples. All other Canadians may be recognized only for their direct form of belonging to the Canadian political community. As part of a recognition struggle, deep diversity is premised on a shallow, nonlayered diversity for some. Deep diversity takes on this line-drawing character when it is used as a trump in the struggle for national recognition. Otherwise, there is no obvious reason why it should matter to those in Quebec whether or not people in Alberta also have access to deep diversity.

Another difficulty is that English Canada is hardly uniform in its desire for national uniformity. And yet Taylor puts great emphasis on uniformity in the approach to belonging of English Canadians, as if this is what all English Canadians really desired. According to Taylor,

> We face a challenge to our very conception of diversity. Many of the people who rallied around the Charter and multiculturalism

to reject the distinct society are proud of their acceptance of diversity – and in some respects rightly so. What is enshrined here is what one might call first-level diversity. There are great differences in culture and outlook and background in a population that nevertheless shares the same idea of what it is to belong to Canada. Their patriotism or manner of belonging is uniform, whatever their differences, and this is felt to be a necessity if the country is to hold together.[42]

Because it is set within a recognition struggle, the asymmetrical federalism required by deep diversity also requires symmetry among English Canadians and their provinces. Deep diversity does not reject English Canadian demands for symmetry, but shifts this symmetry onto English Canada itself.

Some English Canadians may very well desire a uniform basis of belonging, of the first-level type Taylor describes, but this is a matter of great contestation among English Canadians too. While Taylor calls for a "plurality of ways of belonging," his notion of deep diversity consolidates the ways of belonging into two static categories – a duality rather than a fluid plurality. Yet some English Canadians want access to deep diversity too, including recognition of their communitarian, national (provincial, regional, etc.) bases of belonging.

Few would doubt that Canadians in different provinces and regions have developed different ways of belonging to the Canadian political community, with different meanings attached to their provincial membership vis-à-vis their Canadian citizenship and so on. The presence of asymmetrical attachments is thus not at issue, since they have necessarily existed throughout Canadian history. Instead the issue is the equal recognition of these asymmetrical attachments, according to a specific configuration.

One of the ironies of the Calgary Declaration is that, while it rejects the recognition of asymmetry sought by Quebec, in doing so it provides greater space for multiple assymetries in practice. Similarly, even had they omitted a distinct society clause, the result of the Meech Lake and Charlottetown Accords would have been more complex and open to multiplicity than Taylor's dualistic understanding (with only two distinct and static routes of belonging).

In contrast to Taylor's proposal, a more fluid and complex form of deep diversity would allow for variations *within* English Canada as well. Yes, a Québécois might connect to the federal level via his or her province in a different way than an Ontarian, as Taylor suggests. But an Ontarian might also connect differently from a Nova Scotian, who might in turn belong differently from an Albertan, and so on. And each may desire recognition for his or her distinctive layer of belonging. Yet deep diversity precludes variations in belonging to Canada *among* English Canadians.

The next chapter examines an alternative possibility, pursued by Will Kymlicka and others. Perhaps Taylor's aim with deep diversity is in fact to make a space not just for Québécois nationalism but also for English Canadian nationalism.

chapter five

Nationalisms Disentangled: The New Treason of the Intellectuals

> This is what I call *la nouvelle trahison des clercs:* this self-deluding passion of a large segment of our thinking population for throwing themselves headlong – intellectually and spiritually – into purely escapist pursuits.
> – Pierre Trudeau, "New Treason of the Intellectuals"

> **tease** /tiːz/ *v.z.n.* – *v.t.r.* (also *absol.*) ... 2 pick (wool, hair, etc.) into separate fibres ...
> **tease out** separate by disentangling
> – Concise Oxford Dictionary

Recent Canadian history – one might even say Canadian history in general – has been marked by a clash of nationalisms. In response to one manifestation of nationalism deemed problematic, an alternative nationalism is pursued in its place. Most famously, Pierre Trudeau rejected the idea that nations and states need be coterminous and fought against the nationalists in Quebec.[1] Throughout his political career, he cultivated pan-Canadian nationalism instead. It worked – in English Canada at least. In one of the most ironic developments of Canadian history, Trudeau's alternative came to reflect the kind of nation-state ideology he had earlier rejected.[2] This provided further nourishment for the nationalists in Quebec and, of course, exacerbated the impasse of Canadian unity. Instead of constituting a people, or a stronger sense of unity, Trudeau's pivotal participation in the Canadian conversation led to a series of recognition struggles polarized around nationalist and identitarian lines. Apparently, Canadians have not yet realized that the strategy of combating one type of nationalism with another produces yet more nationalism. And so the Canadian conversation continues.

Nationalisms Disentangled

In an attempt to combat the pan-Canadian nationalism of Trudeau, a number of English Canadian intellectuals have put forward yet another nationalist alternative centred on English Canada. This alternative has taken different forms in the work of Philip Resnick, Ian Angus, and many others, but an especially interesting formulation is put forward by Will Kymlicka in his book *Finding Our Way*.[3] For Kymlicka, pan-Canadian nationalism cannot coexist with Québécois nationalism (or Aboriginal nationalism for that matter) because it is driven to subsume them. The trick, then, is to disentangle these nationalisms; Kymlicka's strategy is to shift English Canadian political identification away from a pan-Canadian nation toward a focus on English Canada itself. With the development of an English Canadian nation, the drive for recognition and community can be pursued simultaneously and compatibly by English Canada, Quebec, and Aboriginal peoples. Indeed, the various nationalisms would be mutually reinforcing.

In this chapter, I explore the dangers of developing English Canadian nationalism in this way, especially its aim of disentangling the identities and groupings integral to the Canadian conversation. Even if English Canadian nationalism were to clarify the Canadian conversation, there is reason to believe that such nationalism would merely displace some of the most troubling characteristics of the current impasse to another level – *within* English Canada.

The Theft of (English) Canadian National Enjoyment

In Chapter 4, I depicted how the Calgary Declaration is driven to reject the kind of asymmetry entailed by deep diversity. To explore this further, consider English Canada's equality discourse as an expression of resentment. According to Michael Ignatieff, "The mood of English Canada has settled into a *single angry demand:* enough is enough. This anger is focused not just on Quebec, but also on aboriginal peoples and other rights-claimants. Enough concessions, enough negotiations, enough rights already. There is a new sympathy for symmetrical federalism: equal rights for all provinces and all individuals; no special status for anybody."[4] Given the presence of Quebec, Aboriginal peoples, and other minorities, English Canada has had to follow the route of a weak nationalism, defined by diversity, thereby forgoing dreams of a singular and common national identity.

In psychoanalytic terms, following Slavoj Žižek, we might say that English Canadians suffer from a theft of national enjoyment, having sacrificed their authentic nationalist dreams and instead, out of necessity, pursued an embrace of diversity as a route to national unity.[5] Even so, this embrace of diversity has never been deemed adequate by the Québécois or Aboriginal peoples, who insist on moving beyond the patronizing idea of their diversity as a "gift" (as the Calgary Declaration puts it) to pursue stronger forms of differentiation. Their weak nationalism apparently taken advantage of repeatedly, proponents of pan-Canadian nationalism pursue equal provinces as a way of drawing nationalist lines, as if to say, we English Canadians have been willing to sacrifice much of our national enjoyment in order to make a place for you, yet you cannot expect us to give up on our nationalist dreams altogether.[6] The insistence on equal provinces is an attempt to limit and even downgrade Quebec's demand to be recognized as distinct, to destroy Quebec's route to national enjoyment.

To deal with the "single angry demand" of English Canada, Ignatieff speaks of the need for balancing acts of recognition: "Recognition is a two-way street. National unity, therefore, depends on equality of rights and equality of recognition: minorities recognize majorities; majorities recognize minorities."[7] Nobody disagrees with the importance of mutual recognition. However, the very idea of recognition as a "two-way street" suggests discrete groupings on either end that must each recognize the other in order to be recognized. This does not happen in a satisfactory way because, in this case, the self-recognition of "English Canada" is itself a matter of contestation; there is no "single" demand from English Canada, angry or otherwise. According to Ignatieff, "We do not inhabit the same historical reality. And it is time we did. For two generations, English Canada has asked, with earnest respect, 'What does Quebec want?' It is time for English Canada to say who *we* are and what *our* country is. The answer is: we are a partnership of nations, a community of peoples united in common citizenship and rights. We do possess a common history, and like it or not, we had better begin sharing a common truth."[8]

Although Ignatieff's formulation situates Quebec and "English Canada" on either ends of a two-way recognition street, many English Canadians continue to refuse an English Canadian nationality. This is not because they have refused the "we" question; instead, it is *because* they already have their own answer. The multinational premise of Ignatieff's two-way street of recognition leaves many of them misrecognized. This is why the Calgary Declaration's path of equal uniqueness and Taylor's deep diversity are mutually exclusive. Instead of displacing the opposition, deep diversity reinforces it because it grants recognition to Quebec and Aboriginal peoples while necessarily misrecognizing (English) Canada's pan-Canadian conception. Only in this recurring pattern of disagreement and misrecognition do we find anything approximating a common history – or common truth.

Taylor points toward another way of approaching the issue, however. In attempting to destroy Quebec's route to national enjoyment, English Canada destroys its own. *Yet English Canada need not make this sacrifice.* If it recognizes Quebec as a distinct nation, English Canada may then be recognized as a nation in the same way. English Canada can have its nation too. While Taylor does not elaborate on this approach, others have proceeded along these lines.

Kymlicka's English Canadian Nationalism

Although Kymlicka approves of Taylor's proposal for deep diversity and asymmetrical federalism, he understands the challenges involved in getting English Canada to agree to it. Since asymmetry is premised on a multinational conception of Canada, it clashes with pan-Canadian nationalism. Kymlicka argues that "while English-speaking Canadians often express their opposition to special status in the language of equality, this concern grows out of an even deeper concern with nationhood. That is, English-speaking Canadians interpret 'equality' as requiring identical rights and powers for all provinces because any other conception of equality would undermine their sense of a common Canadian nationhood."[9]

Kymlicka thus believes that it is necessary to target the symmetrical conception of citizenship and federalism pursued by pan-Canadian nationalists: "To persuade English-speaking Canadians to endorse the multination conception of Canada, therefore, we need to directly confront and challenge the ideal of a unitary Canadian nationality ... [We need to] show not only that the dream of a common national identity is impossible to realize, but also that it is not worth aspiring to."[10]

Rather than simply disregard the energies of pan-Canadian nationalism, Kymlicka's approach is to shift its terms by replacing it with a stronger, more developed English Canadian identity. As soon as English Canadians begin to see themselves as a coherent national community, he argues, they will be far less likely to reject a multinational understanding of Canada. They will take a less antagonistic stance toward the differentiated ways of Quebec and Aboriginal peoples precisely because these differences will reflect the horizon of the English Canadian community.

To be clear, Kymlicka is wary of presenting English Canada in nationalist terms at all, preferring to speak of a common English Canadian identity. Still, he does use the word "nation," and it is difficult to imagine English Canadians considering themselves as merely an "identity" within the context of a "multinational" partnership with Quebec and Aboriginal peoples. Whatever language is used, we are speaking of the substitution of one form of nationalism (pan-Canadian) by another (English Canadian). As Kymlicka notes, the price of this trade-off is the "dream of a single Canadian nation."[11]

Those pursuing the development of English Canadian nationalism offer a range of justifications. Some rationales are of the traditional-left nationalist variety, emphasizing the necessity of a strong English Canada in order to develop alternatives to free trade, US economic power, and global capital generally. For example, as Reg Whitaker points out in relation to the 1988 free trade election, "Freed of the rhetoric of National Unity, there are elements in English Canada that could offer a stronger, rather than weaker, basis for national identification in a Canada-without-Quebec."[12] Relatedly, Kymlicka argues that, as soon as English Canada develops a sense of itself as a nation and is no longer opposed to asymmetry, it will be in a far better position to maintain a strong central government, even as Quebec assumes certain additional powers. This would stand in contrast to the present situation, in which demands by Quebec for more powers are met by making these powers available to all the provinces, thus encouraging decentralization in order to preserve symmetry. Accordingly, Kymlicka says asymmetry "would, in effect, enable English-speaking Canadians to act more forcefully in defence of their common interests and national identity."[13] As important as these economic and social justifications are, they are secondary to the aims of the Canadian conversation.

In the context of the Canadian conversation, the main rationale for the development of English Canadian nationalism is that English Canada must recognize itself in order to recognize Quebec. Over the course of Canadian history, variations of Kymlicka's proposal have been put forward by many Québécois and English Canadian intellectuals who have expressed frustration at the lack of a coherent English Canadian identity with which Quebec may enter into a dialogue of mutual recognition.[14] For example, André Laurendeau once asked, "Is it possible to imagine that to protect itself against the troubles in Quebec, English Canada might forge a new sense of unity and learn to define itself once again? Then we would have *someone to talk to* and they could talk back, and the battle would be fierce. But that would be better, it seems to me, than messing around in the kind of swamp we are all bogged down in now."[15] To provide Quebec with a conversation partner, Taylor and Kymlicka make their case for English Canadian nationalism.

A Conversation Partner for Quebec

Of course, no one proposing the development of English Canadian nationalism is unaware of the difficulty of bringing such a national identity into existence. One immediate hurdle is the national enjoyment many English Canadians (and a few Québécois too) gain from embracing or containing Quebec ("My Canada includes Quebec!"). Trudeau is often blamed (or celebrated) for this situation. Through pan-Canadian policies such as bilingualism, multiculturalism, and, of course, the Charter of Rights and Freedoms, Trudeau attempted to dull Canadian dualism. Instead of a distinct English

Canadian conversation partner, Quebec has had to put up with English Canada's pan-Canadian embrace. Much scholarly discussion constructs Trudeau as having fabricated an artificial and inauthentic pan-Canadian nation that is untrue to Canada's origins or fails to actualize its dreams. As Whitaker points out, any proposal for the development of English Canada will be resisted strongly by the "Ottawa National Unity industry," which will insist "on the unbending assumption that there is a Canada, which by definition includes Quebec, but that English Canada has no legitimate existence." Still, Whitaker argues, "English Canadians should ignore these admonitions and get on with the task of *defining themselves* as a community, with or without Quebec."[16]

Trudeau's nationalism has been criticized for "misconceiving Canada" by Kenneth McRoberts and as representing the "end of a Canadian dream" by Guy Laforest.[17] The artificiality of pan-Canadian nationalism is then contrasted with some notion of English Canadian authenticity. Thus, Whitaker argues that it is time for English Canada to "find its own authentic voice."[18] Similarly, Ian Angus has spoken of the need to develop English Canadian self-consciousness: "Instead of discovering ourselves mainly on the rebound from our encounters with others, we may also define ourselves through the coming to self-consciousness of the cultural and political identity of English Canada itself, through our own definition of our national identity. In this way we may at last begin to appreciate the claims and desires of the other two main groups."[19] But how else do we discover ourselves, except on the rebound from such encounters?

Part of the difficulty of the Canadian conversation is that the "sides" of the debate do not correspond to the national categories in dispute. Instead, the debate often polarizes precisely around the meaning of these national categories. Though everyone agrees that the categories overlap, they disagree over how or to what extent. The Canadian conversation would, of course, be much clearer if the boundaries of these categories were clarified through the sort of disentanglement dreamed of by those pursuing English Canadian nationalism. Indeed, once the national categories were certain or fixed, the Canadian conversation would be a formality. It is far easier to negotiate the relationship between distinct entities than to negotiate relationships without such agreement.

The Pursuit of English Canadian Authenticity

Even given the development of a multinational Canada of the sort Kymlicka proposes, some arrangements concerning the relationship between each nation and Canada as a whole would still be necessary. Presumably, there would be a much greater openness to forms of differentiated citizenship between the nations and greater flexibility for each nation to pursue different paths and different ways of belonging to Canada as a whole. After all, this is the rationale for the multinational alternative. Still, Kymlicka remains concerned with the basis of unity among the nations of a multinational Canada. He asks, "Is multinational federalism a stable form of political organization? Or is it too fragmented and divided to be capable of producing the sort of allegiance, trust, and solidarity among its citizens that a stable democracy requires?"[20] While Kymlicka downplays the extent of unity required in a multinational context, he is nevertheless concerned to discover ways of guarding against fragmentation. He argues that Canadians cannot look to their history, since this tends to divide them, and nor can they expect to unite around "shared values." Instead, the route to unity must be found in some form of shared identity. Kymlicka realizes that this is a rather vague concept and so he discusses a range of factors that might help to cultivate a shared identity. Remarkably, he eventually settles on Webber's notion of the Canadian conversation and Taylor's belief that Canadians might take pride in the idea of deep diversity itself.[21]

For his part, Taylor is well aware that many in English Canada will reject deep diversity in the belief it will lead to disunity and fragmentation. He asks, "Is this [deep diversity] utopian? Could people ever come to see their country this way? Could they even find it exciting and an object of pride that they belong to a country that allows deep diversity? Pessimists say no, because they do not see how such a country could have a sense of unity. The model of citizenship has to be uniform, or people would have no sense of belonging to the same polity."[22] Far from dismissing the problem of unity, Taylor argues that those who attempt to pursue unity through a forced symmetry of equal citizens and provinces are far more likely to cultivate fragmentation.[23] For Taylor, deep diversity is the best way of counteracting fragmentation and thus ensuring unity. His theorizing takes on a teleological flavour here; deep diversity implies a vision of the Canadian political community as an organic ensemble within which the dialectic of unity-in-difference may play out.[24]

Particularly notable is that Kymlicka finds it necessary to continue the search for a basis of cohesion. The whole purpose of Kymlicka's proposal is to get beyond the current symmetry/asymmetry divide. But as long as unity remains imperative, at some level, there will seemingly always be attempts to define the whole, and there is good reason to believe that one nation's vision will clash with that of others, replicating the antagonisms that we have now.

Even assuming that English Canadians can be coaxed into abandoning their quest for a pan-Canadian nation in favour of the pursuit of an English

Canadian identity or nation, this proposal has a number of troubling implications. Of course, *any* proposal that encourages the development of nationalism is troubling and, hence, Kymlicka himself proceeds very cautiously.

How will the "common interests" of English Canadians be defined, and precisely who will be in a position to "act more forcefully in defence" of them (to recall Kymlicka's phrasing)? The progressive answer to these questions is that the common interests would be defined and acted upon inclusively and democratically. Yet there are other proposals for English Canadian nationalism rooted in quite different motivations; these proposals reason not that Quebec and Aboriginal peoples have been *suppressed,* but rather that they have been continually *appeased* to the detriment of English Canada.

A good deal of the resentment expressed by English Canadians toward Quebec and other minorities is driven by the idea that, given the need to accommodate Quebec in order to keep it in Canada, English Canadians have always had to refrain from pursuing their own national vision, making them weak and apologetic. Richard Gwyn has argued this case.[25]

The willingness of English Canadians to abandon their passive pan-Canadian dreams would presumably hinge on their being able to pursue dreams of a single and unified English Canadian nation instead, without the hindrances of large minorities. This is obviously not Kymlicka's motivation, but one can anticipate that these are the grounds, if any, on which English Canadians would embrace a multinational Canada. And one can imagine what *this* English Canadian nationalism might look like once unleashed. "Finally," English Canadians would be able to pursue their "authentic" national vision without having to temper it so as not to appear overbearing to minorities. Mechanisms of English Canadian moderation could be put aside in the vigorous pursuit of English Canadian authenticity.[26]

The pursuit of English Canadian nationalism can also be understood in another way. To the extent that an English Canadian identity is now implicit in pan-Canadian nationalism, this identity cannot be presented as "English" Canadian without undercutting its own basis. The identity of the English Canadian nation lies, ostensibly, in its nonidentity. Hence, Philip Resnick speaks of English Canada as "a nation that dare not speak its name."[27] The great danger of the proposal for English Canadian nationalism is that once English Canada does "speak its name," it ceases to exist in the form that we have known it. The decisive enunciation "English Canada" amounts to a break with the past and, as a result, English Canada becomes something altogether different from the old (pan-Canadian) English Canada (which was feeble and apologetic in the form of the mosaic, or which saw itself as such). Presumably, the new English Canada would be in a better position to act with greater clarity in its national pursuits.

Even if the English Canadian nation were not defined by extremists, but by politicians and intellectuals concerned with social justice and self-determination, the identity and unity of the English Canadian nation would still be at issue. English Canadians, having accepted deep diversity, might successfully disentangle their recognition claims from those of Quebec and Aboriginal peoples, but similar problems would remain within English Canada (as they would within Quebec and Aboriginal communities as well). In order to pursue the sorts of "common interests" that Kymlicka speaks of, some identifiable form of unity would be needed. The problem of diversity would not disappear with the shift away from pan-Canadian nationalism; it would only be displaced to another level. The disentanglement of English Canada from Quebec and Aboriginal peoples would merely shift anxieties about diversity to *within* each of the three nations. Recall that deep diversity emphasizes and clarifies the distinctions between the nations while resisting variation within them. Deep diversity reinforces asymmetrical differences between categories of people while cultivating a basis of uniformity or symmetry within each category.

Of course, scholars such as Kymlicka, Whitaker, Angus, and Resnick will insist that the new English Canadian community would embrace diversity and pluralism, not assimilation or uniformity, but the anxieties surrounding the question of diversity in a future English Canada have already been expressed in the writings of English Canadian intellectuals. While Resnick views multiculturalism as central to any future conception of English Canada, he notes that "there comes a point beyond which multiculturalism could become a threat to the viability of an English-Canadian nationality."[28] This comment is troubling, and not less so because it is familiar in the current context of pan-Canadian nationalism.

Given the emphasis on unity *within*, it is not too difficult to imagine English Canadian politics polarizing between those asserting some form of pluralist unity through diversity (i.e., differentiated citizenship) and those asserting a stronger form of unity through equal treatment or some other binding mechanism. As long as the "solutions" to the "problem" operate on the terrain of unity (whether national or subnational), this polarizing dynamic will be replicated. Anxieties about cohesion and fragmentation will continue to be expressed, as will concerns about the character and identity of the nation. There will be a search for some set of values or practices or ways of belonging common to all English Canadians. Attempts will be made to suppress certain differences in order to bind everyone together into a cohesive whole, leaving some groups marginalized, excluded, and misrecognized.

It is impossible to know for certain what English Canadian nationalism would look like in practice, but it will probably resemble the situation many Canadians have been trying to escape. The English Canadian alternative merely shifts the problem from one unit of national identity to another, because the problem is not limited to the imperative to *pan-Canadian* unity but relates to the more general nationalist preoccupation with identity and unity.

chapter six

The Arithmetic of Canadian Citizenship

> The unasked question, which remains unanswered when the goal of autonomy crowds out togetherness, or when nationalism pushes a common citizenship to the margins of consciousness is "What will hold us together?" Is there any common "we" group to which we all belong? Is a shared geography and propinquity enough to sustain feelings of responsibility for each other that transcend the historical Aboriginal/non-Aboriginal divide that we have inherited?
>
> These are central questions that recur in a small body of literature written mainly by political scientists. Their concern is with the whole. They assume the necessity of a degree of common civic identity as one of the glues that hold the country together. They believe that the degree of concern we have for each other is a function of the strength of the common "we" group to which we belong.
>
> –Alan Cairns, *Citizens Plus*

The 1969 *Statement of the Government of Canada on Indian Policy,* known as the White Paper, is one of only a handful of Canadian public policy documents that, decades later, carries resonance beyond narrow policy and academic circles.[1] That the White Paper was so soundly rejected makes this resonance especially interesting. Much like Lord Durham's report, the White Paper has become a symbol of the assimilationist option that Canadians decided *not* to take.

By exploring the logic of the White Paper and the debates surrounding it, this chapter builds on the existing scholarship in order to better understand contemporary debates.[2] To contextualize the White Paper properly, I begin by examining a major report released three years earlier, *A Survey of the Contemporary Indians of Canada* (known as the Hawthorn Report).[3] The Hawthorn Report pursued a form of Aboriginal differentiation, in contrast to the

White Paper, which rejected the historical differentiation of Aboriginal people, using the language of equal citizenship. This chapter probes the problems created by the citizens equal versus "citizens plus" framing, especially for those struggling to transform Aboriginal/non-Aboriginal relations. Historically, this debate has drawn, and continues to draw, Aboriginal peoples into structuring their struggles in terms of how they relate to the broader Canadian political community. Doing so funnels their struggles into a set of false dilemmas over questions of unity and away from issues of self-governance and justice. Struggles for justice, equality, and democratic governance are routed into debates over the "ties that bind" Canadian citizens together.

Rather than attempt an answer to the question of citizens equal or citizens plus, my aim is to understand its dynamics and lingering effects. Even as the relationship between Aboriginal and non-Aboriginal peoples has transformed in so many ways over the last three decades – with the Charter, Royal Commission on Aboriginal Peoples, Nunavut, and the Nisga'a Treaty – we have continued to see the replaying of this polarizing debate. The debate not only continues as part of the Canadian conversation but takes place increasingly among non-Aboriginal Canadians, much to the concern of Alan Cairns.

The Hawthorn Report: From Citizens Minus to Citizens Plus

In the early 1960s, the media began presenting disturbing images of the appalling conditions on reserves and among Aboriginal people living in the cities. Given the anomalous character of this situation in the context of Canada's increasingly wealthy liberal-democratic society, the so-called Indian problem became a major concern of Canadian politicians and bureaucrats; one important outcome was the Hawthorn Report. Commissioned in 1963 by the federal government, the two-volume report represents the findings of a group of Canadian academics centred at the University of British Columbia. While the tone of the Hawthorn Report is rather measured and analytical, the authors' moral outrage over the poverty and despair pervasive among Aboriginal people in Canada is easily discerned, and evident throughout is the desire to construct a realistic set of solutions to this situation.

The Hawthorn Report is best known for the phrase "citizens plus," coined by Alan Cairns, then a junior political scientist at UBC and the main author of the political sections of volume 1. It is worth analyzing this intriguing phrase, which the report goes to great lengths to defend: "The right [to be regarded as 'citizens plus'] derives from promises made to them, from expectations they were encouraged to hold, and from the simple fact that they once occupied and used a country to which others came to gain enormous wealth in which the Indians have shared little."[4] While the report acknowledges that, for many, the word "plus" is in tension with the "egalitarian" character of Canadian society, it says that "the reverse status Indians have held, as citizens *minus*, which is equally repugnant to a strongly egalitarian society, has been tolerated for a long time ... By every calculation they have been disprivileged and low-cost citizens up to the present time and many services will need to be increased for them before they catch up."[5] As is evident from the phrase "catch up," the "plus" is designed to reverse the historical disadvantages of Aboriginal people. For this reason, where its effects may be deleterious to the interests of Aboriginal people, the "plus" is to be bracketed in favour of equal treatment.[6]

In institutional terms, the "plus" is reflected most strongly in the report's recommendation for retaining the Indian Act and the Indian Affairs Branch.[7] The report proposes that Indian Affairs assume the role of "national conscience" so as to facilitate socioeconomic equality "between Indians and Whites."[8] This insistence on maintaining Indian Affairs and other institutions of Aboriginal governance such as the Indian Act itself was controversial, since these institutions were widely viewed as paternalistic and backward in their treatment of Aboriginal people.[9] The report justifies retaining Indian Affairs on the basis that Aboriginal people were not yet competent to initiate on their own the sorts of economic and social improvements required.[10] At least initially, the "plus" component is to be designed and directed by federal bureaucrats rather than by Aboriginal people themselves. Indeed, the "plus" is to be in effect in precisely those areas where they are believed to be too inexperienced or simply incapable of pursuing their own needs.[11] While the report presents the "plus" as an Aboriginal right, its framing is surprisingly paternalistic.

This paternalism appears contradictory, yet the "plus" is designed as an alternative route to the norms of Canadian citizenship – not as a means for maintaining or encouraging separate Aboriginal cultures or communities. The "plus" encourages separate institutions only where these would raise the socioeconomic condition of Aboriginal people to approximate those of other Canadian citizens. In its opening pages, the Hawthorn Report states, "The whole direction of the Report argues towards increasing the scope for decision by Indians and this includes a decision either to reside in separate cultural communities or to leave them temporarily or permanently."[12] It emphasizes not simply the right to make such choices but rather the *ability* to make meaningful choices, so central to liberal citizenship. The report notes, "No choice by Indians, neither to accept nor to reject Canadian values and opportunities, can have a sequel of purposeful action and successful result unless they have certain capacities to sustain it."[13] Given this, to suggest that the "plus" involves encouraging citizenship differentiation for the sake of differentiation would be to misinterpret seriously its purpose.[14]

The report thus opposes *forced* assimilation. Yet it endorses, at least implicitly, a milder form of assimilation on the grounds that the choices of Aboriginal people (i.e., to integrate or pursue separation) can have real meaning only within a framework of liberal citizenship, which the "plus" is designed to cultivate.

The emphasis of the report is not "citizens *plus*" but instead "*citizens* plus." Even though the word "plus" is the inevitable focus of attention in the debate surrounding it, it is the word "citizens" that propels the report forward. Because they are citizens, the disadvantaged position of Aboriginal people can no longer be tolerated; because they are citizens, Aboriginal people have the right to equality of opportunity. The word "citizens" defines the goal, and the word "plus" is merely a means to achieve that goal, through state-directed differential treatment in certain limited areas.

This liberal citizenship framework, which is to allow Aboriginal people to make meaningful choices, is far from neutral. In particular, Canadian citizenship is explicitly racialized, and the report contrasts Aboriginal peoples as an undifferentiated totality, as the other to the white Canadian basis of citizenship. The report is preoccupied with sorting out how this other can best fit into Canada's liberal citizenship regime. Therefore, although the "plus" is a form of differentiation, it is differentiation as a vehicle of assimilation to racialized liberal citizenship norms. Paradoxically, the report justifies this route on the grounds that only from within this liberal framework can Aboriginal people make real decisions about the cultural path they wish to follow. This was the central tension of the report – this progressive *desire* to help assimilation along, without forcing it, so that Aboriginal people could then be in a position to reject it if, regrettably, they decided to do so. This tension resurfaced three decades later when Alan Cairns revisited the question, as I will discuss below.

Like most such reports, the Hawthorn Report was effectively shelved soon after its release, yet its "citizens plus" logic has helped to shape the debate ever since.

Trudeau's White Paper on Indian Policy: Citizens Equal

An important component of Trudeau's "Just Society" initiative, the *Statement of the Government of Canada on Indian Policy* was unveiled by Jean Chrétien, then the Minister of Indian Affairs and Northern Development, in June 1969. Although the Trudeau government had promised to place Aboriginal issues on its policy agenda, and although it had undertaken a series of consultations with Aboriginal bands throughout Canada, the release of the White Paper was a shock to Aboriginal leaders. Sally Weaver has described the process of developing the White Paper in great detail, arguing that the consultations had little connection with the development of the policy, which was constructed in great secrecy by a network of long-time bureaucrats working with Chrétien and Trudeau in the Department of Indian Affairs and Northern Development.[15] The aggressive and heavy-handed attempt to impose the policy on Aboriginal people represents the backdrop for the analysis that follows.

Just thirteen pages long, the White Paper presents five central principles:

1. that the legislative and constitutional bases of discrimination be removed;
2. that there be positive recognition by everyone of the unique contribution of Indian culture to Canadian life;
3. that services come through the same channels and from the same government agencies for all Canadians;
4. that those who are furthest behind be helped most;
5. that control of Indian lands be transferred to the Indian people.[16]

The central thrust of the White Paper revolves around the first principle, eliminating legal and constitutional discrimination, which amounts to the termination of the legal distinction between Aboriginal and non-Aboriginal people in Canada. This would have entailed the unilateral tearing-up of the historical treaties. In their place, the White Paper proposes a version of undifferentiated citizenship grounded in the legal and constitutional equality of all citizens: "Services ought not to flow from separate agencies established to serve particular groups, especially not to groups that are identified ethnically. Separate but equal services do not provide truly equal treatment. Treatment has not been equal in the case of Indians and their communities."[17]

This application of the principle of equal treatment would have required a significant shift in the governance of Aboriginal peoples in Canada. The treaties, the Indian Act, and all the specialized federal agencies that deal with Aboriginal people (especially Indian Affairs) would all need to be eliminated. Reserve lands would no longer be held in trust by the Crown for Aboriginal peoples, as is required by the treaties and the Indian Act, but would instead be dealt with by individual bands as each saw fit. Furthermore, for the first time Aboriginal people would be integrated into the federal system in that all social and educational programs would be administered to Aboriginal people by the provinces, as they are to other Canadian citizens.

In contrast to the Hawthorn Report's approach, the White Paper emphasizes "the simple reality that the separate legal status of Indians and the policies which have flowed from it have kept the Indian people apart from and behind other Canadians."[18] Throughout, the White Paper argues that since the legal distinction between Aboriginal and non-Aboriginal people has disadvantaged Aboriginal people in multiple ways, justice demands that this legal distinction be eliminated. Rather than actually demonstrating this point, the White Paper relies on a fairly commonsensical connection. Aboriginal people are disadvantaged according to virtually every social, economic, and political indicator; at the same time, Aboriginal people have always been legally differentiated from other Canadians, most notably through the treaties, the Indian Act, and the role of Indian Affairs. Social, economic, and political disparities are presented as following logically – in a cause and effect relationship – from all the long-standing legal and constitutional distinctions: "Canada cannot seek the just society and keep discriminatory legislation on its statute books. The Government believes this to be self-evident."[19] The only route to justice and equality involves equal treatment.

As adamant as the White Paper is about the elimination of legal distinctions, it does make limited space for differential treatment based on its fourth principle, that "those who are furthest behind be helped most." In the text of the White Paper, this principle falls under the heading "enriched services," where it is acknowledged that "equality before the law and in programs and services does not necessarily result in equality in social and economic conditions."[20] Special treatment may thus be necessary in certain limited cases after all. Still, the White Paper emphasizes, many of the economic problems faced by Aboriginal people are in fact regional in nature, so that "in many situations, the problems of Indians are similar to those faced by their non-Indian neighbours."[21] Presumably, to the extent that special treatment is necessary, its administration would therefore be regionalized – as opposed to racialized – wherever possible.

Aboriginal leaders rejected the White Paper because they saw it as assimilationist, as an attempt to eliminate Aboriginal cultures and practices, as a form of cultural genocide. This was the dominant understanding of the White Paper upon its release and, over three decades later, similar terms are still used to describe it. For example, according to Alan Cairns, "The White Paper espoused a straightforward assimilationist strategy/philosophy. Its underlying thesis was that separate status contributed to economic backwardness, social isolation, and retrogressive cultural enclaves. The White Paper, in fact, was a late twentieth-century version of the Durham Report of the previous century, with Indians substituted for the backward, unprogressive Quebec peasantry."[22] James Tully shares this assessment: "In 1969 the Prime Minister of Canada, Pierre Trudeau, announced his plan to abolish the treaty system and assimilate all Aboriginal people into the modern Canadian society for the sake of their improvement."[23]

Thus defined, the White Paper has come to represent the path Canadians rejected, as if at a fork in the road. Mere mention of the White Paper serves to funnel complex issues into this either/or, assimilationist/nonassimilationist framing. This clarity is deceptive, of course, and so it is worth exploring the White Paper's strategy further, especially its *similarities* with the Hawthorn Report.

Despite its assimilationist associations, the White Paper mentions difference repeatedly, as illustrated in its first three sentences: "To be an Indian is to be a man, with all a man's needs and abilities. To be an Indian is also to be different. It is to speak different languages, draw different pictures, tell different tales and to rely on a set of values developed in a different world." The White Paper is careful to distinguish these differences, which it affirms, from its real target: differentiation or differential treatment.

The White Paper is an invitation to Aboriginal people to join the Canadian multicultural mosaic, on the premise that their inclusion will make for a more interesting Canadian cultural landscape. Accordingly, it notes, "The Indian contribution to North American society is often overlooked, even by the Indian people themselves ... Too often, the art forms which express the past are preserved, but are inaccessible to most Indian people. This richness can be shared by all Canadians. Indian people must be helped to become aware of their history and heritage in all its forms, and this heritage must be brought before *all* Canadians in all its rich diversity."[24] Without the display of Aboriginal culture in Canada, Canadians would be deprived of the opportunity to admire and appreciate it.

The White Paper's logic proceeds as follows: you ("Indians") must have faith in our ("Canadian") game, the game of equal citizenship, because it is designed to provide you with the space to play your game (the game of being "Indian"). Notice the language: "The Indian people are ... entitled to an equality which preserves and enriches Indian identity and distinction; an equality which stresses Indian participation in its creation and which manifests itself in all aspects of Indian life."[25] Certainly, by manifesting itself "in all aspects of Indian life," equality (as a form of commonality) seems to be in tension with the expression of "Indian identity and distinction." As the White Paper would have it, however, diversity best flourishes within a framework of equality considered as a layer of commonality. It proposes equal treatment as the best hope not for assimilation but instead for the continued vitality of Aboriginal cultures: "The goals of the Indian people cannot be set by others; they must spring from the Indian community itself – but government can create a *framework* within which all persons and groups can seek their own goals."[26] Equality, then, is essential for a multicultural result because it provides individuals with the space necessary for them to express their different cultural traditions as they wish. According to the White Paper, equal treatment represents a third route that explicitly rejects the extremes of separatism or assimilation and instead "offers great opportunity for Canadians to demonstrate that in our open society there is room for the development of people who preserve their different cultures and take pride in their diversity."[27]

If this is what the White Paper means, then it is indeed an assimilationist document to the extent that it entails assimilation to a common framework defined by equal treatment and designed to allow for, and encourage, Aboriginal difference. Diversity is to be encouraged, but only when developed *within* the common framework (or common *limit*) of equal citizenship.

In important respects, then, the approach of the White Paper toward assimilation is not so different from the approach of the Hawthorn Report, except that the Hawthorn Report's common framework of equality is supplemented in certain important areas by forms of differentiation. I have argued that the Hawthorn Report is pragmatic where the question of equal or differential treatment is concerned, favouring whichever mixture works best in specific contexts. The meaning of the contrasting dynamic of the White Paper and its rejection of differential treatment becomes clearer when one looks at what Chrétien and Trudeau were trying to accomplish. Despite its stated objectives, the main problem that the White Paper aims to solve is not the poor socioeconomic condition of Aboriginal people but the threat that their differentiation represents to Canada.

In order to demonstrate this, it is necessary to examine further the White Paper's preoccupation with a common framework of equality. As discussed, the White Paper claims that differential treatment invariably disadvantages the differentiated. Still, this position is superseded by the even stronger claim that – whatever their economic or political effect – legal distinctions are simply intolerable. The language of the White Paper is clear: "The treatment resulting from their different status has been often worse, sometimes equal and occasionally better than that accorded to their fellow citizens. *What matters is that it has been different.*"[28] So the path of differentiation is wrong simply *because it is a different path*. This is a rather striking argument; why should the distinctions themselves matter?

In attempting to eliminate the legal distinction between Aboriginal and non-Aboriginal Canadians, the White Paper aims to cultivate a particular understanding of Canada as a cohesive political community. As with any community, the criteria of belonging are key, and the White Paper presents equal treatment as the central framework of belonging. For example, regarding the proposal that "services come through the same channels and from the same government agencies for all Canadians," the government says, "This is an undeniable part of equality. It has been shown many times that separation of peoples follows from separate services. There can be no argument about the principle of common services. It is a right."[29] Of course, the phrase "there can be no argument" suggests that there very often is argument about such things, in Canada as in other liberal democratic societies. But in stating otherwise, the government is presenting equal citizenship as the basic framework of the Canadian political community, about which there can be – must be – no argument. According to the White Paper, "The Government does not wish to perpetuate policies which carry with them the seeds of disharmony and disunity."[30]

Differentiation threatens the basis of cohesion in Canada and so, on these terms, it must be rejected. In the White Paper, the government is outlining the terms of belonging, and thus deciding who is in and who is out: "This government believes in equality. It believes that all men and women have equal rights. It is determined that all shall be treated fairly and that no one shall be shut out of Canadian life, and especially that no one shall be shut out because of his race."[31] If to be differentiated on legal grounds amounts to being "shut out of Canadian life," then "Canadian life" is defined precisely by the common framework of equality. Those who are not allowed or are unwilling to conform to this framework are beyond the limit of the Canadian political community. Indeed, since they are not part of the community, their existence threatens it.

How do we explain the markedly different tone of the Hawthorn Report, in which the unity of the Canadian community seems to be less of an issue, especially given the differentiation that it insists upon? Perhaps it is because the Hawthorn Report's "plus" – the differentiation of Aboriginal people – is not designed to encourage the sort of separateness that might lead to fragmentation, and thus the question of unity never arises. As I have argued, the "plus" would provide a space for DIAND officials to encourage and monitor the integration of Aboriginal people *into* Canadian citizenship in certain areas where equal treatment alone would not have this desired effect. For the Hawthorn Report, then, the differentiation that comes from the "plus" is not construed as a threat to the cohesion of Canadian citizenship but as a vehicle toward Canadian citizenship. In contrast, the White Paper is willing to take a leap in jettisoning the sort of differentiation central to the "plus" of the Hawthorn Report. Yet it must present an alternative strategy in order to preserve the stability of the Canadian community.

The Red Paper
Aboriginal leaders rejected the White Paper in an aggressive and forceful manner, leading the federal government to withdraw its proposal in the spring

of 1970. Although the Aboriginal reaction took many forms, including grassroots mobilization and public protests, the Indian Chiefs of Alberta presented a particularly significant response to Prime Minister Trudeau a year after the release of the White Paper. Drawing from Harold Cardinal's analysis of the White Paper in his 1969 book, *The Unjust Society*, and adopted eventually by the National Indian Brotherhood, the document was titled, notably, "Citizens Plus," although it came to be known as the Red Paper. It begins with a brief preamble, a "Counter Policy," that argues, "Justice requires that the special history, rights and circumstances of Indian People be recognized."[32] The main theme is a critique of the White Paper's pursuit of formal equality, advocating instead an understanding of equality that involves treating people differently or "specially." The Red Paper notes, "Every group gets special treatment, concessions – even special status. We need and are entitled to special consideration – at the very least we expect that the promises made when we signed the treaties ceding our lands will be honoured."[33]

Rejecting the White Paper's position that differentiation invariably leads to disadvantage, the Red Paper notes that it is the paternalistic Indian Act, and not the treaties themselves, that has long disadvantaged Aboriginal people. The importance of the treaties is emphasized throughout, and the federal government is condemned for attempting to unilaterally eliminate these products of negotiation and mutual agreement.

The Red Paper frames its response to the White Paper by using the Hawthorn language of "citizens plus"; indeed, it begins by quoting the Hawthorn Report. As one would expect, in contrast to the Hawthorn Report, "Citizens Plus" emphasizes self-governance as a necessary first step. Still, in adopting the notion of citizens plus, the Indian Chiefs of Alberta make a point of emphasizing that they take its "citizens" element very seriously. They argue that their different ways of living (i.e., the "plus") can operate *within* the Canadian context as long as Canada makes sufficient space for diversity and pluralism: "The cultures of the Indian peoples are old and colourful strands in that Canadian fabric of diversity. We want our children to learn our ways, our history, our customs, and our traditions. Everyone should recognize that Indians have contributed much to the Canadian community. When we signed the treaties we promised to be good and loyal subjects of the Queen. The record is clear – we kept our promises."[34] As this statement illustrates, the Indian Chiefs of Alberta emphasize their desire for the maintenance of both their Aboriginal identities and their continued place within the Canadian political community. In rejecting the attempt to impose equality in a uniform manner, the Red Paper follows the Hawthorn Report in blending equality ("citizens") and difference ("plus").

There is a further element to this, for the Red Paper's use of the language of "citizens plus" reinforces the development of counterunities. The White Paper attempts to impose unity through equality, and this generates a counterunity through Aboriginal difference. Many scholars and commentators have argued that the White Paper constructed a national Aboriginal consciousness that had not existed previously, or at least not to the same degree. For example, according to Sally Weaver, "Indians responded to the policy with a resounding nationalism unparalleled in Canadian history."[35] Similarly, J.R. Miller argues, "In their uniformly hostile reaction to it [the White Paper], Indian leaders found a basis for a pan-Canadian unity they had long sought but failed to achieve ... The white paper had given them a common enemy against which to mobilize, and the prime minister's retreat had encouraged their troops."[36]

On 4 June 1970, the federal government withdrew the White Paper from any further consideration. Trudeau met with the Indian Association of Alberta and the National Indian Brotherhood and said:

> I'm sure that we were very naïve in some of the statements we made in the paper. We had perhaps the prejudices of small "l" liberals, and white men at that, who thought that equality meant the same law for everybody, and that's why as a result of this we said, "Well, let's abolish the *Indian Act* and make Indians citizens of Canada like everyone else. And let's let Indians dispose of their lands just like every other Canadian" ... But we have learnt in the process that perhaps we were a bit too theoretical, we were a bit too abstract.[37]

In generating a counternationalism, the White Paper appears to have failed in its purpose. For Mary Ellen Turpel, "Trudeau can only take credit for shocking Aboriginal peoples into action years ago – not for finding answers."[38] Nevertheless, interesting here is the manner in which the White Paper produced this counternationalism and oriented it to the logic of the Canadian conversation. The White Paper does not simply precede the Red Paper – indeed, White *produces* Red.

Furthermore, as is common with nationalist movements, this counternationalism itself became concerned with its own unity in order to accentuate and strengthen its difference. As an illustration of this, one of the most notable arguments in the Red Paper came in response to the White Paper's proposal that "those who are furthest behind should be helped most." The Red Paper stated, "We do not want different treatment for different tribes.

These promises of enriched services are bribes to get us to accept the rest of the Policy. The Federal Government is trying to divide us Indian people so it can conquer us by saying that poorer reserves will be helped most."[39]

Putting aside the question of whether the White Paper intended to divide Aboriginal peoples, this statement seems to undermine the initial justification for Aboriginal differentiation. Yet, at another level, it demonstrates that the basis of difference – the "plus" or special treatment – must itself be uniform. In other words, Aboriginal people must remain *differentiated,* and, additionally, they must all remain *differentiated in the same way.* This language is reinforced throughout the Red Paper, which constantly emphasizes the unity of Aboriginal peoples, or at least treaty Indians. The White Paper's attempt to create unity through equality not only generated a counterresponse that asserts difference, but a difference that takes the form of a counter*unity,* a unified difference: red versus white.

Cairns and the Contemporary Debate

In the three and a half decades since the White Paper was rejected, relations between Aboriginal and non-Aboriginal peoples have been transformed, especially in political, legal, and constitutional terms. Aboriginal organizations are now far better organized and more influential, and their struggles have a much higher profile. Perhaps most notably, the position of differentiation was constitutionally entrenched in the form of section 35 of the Charter of Rights and Freedoms, wherein "existing aboriginal treaty rights" were "recognized and affirmed." Remarkably, by the mid-1980s, Douglas Sanders considered the rejection of the equal citizenship position for Aboriginals so strong that he could write, "The general acceptance of Indian special status in Canada is clear. In the post-war period it is the dominant theme in national law and policy under both Conservative and Liberal governments. The White Paper on Indian policy of 1969 was a brief exception. All three national parties officially support the recognition of Indian rights and decry the failures of past governmental policies. No federal or provincial politicians can be identified in Canada today who publicly oppose Indian special status as such."[40]

Within just a few years, however, such opposition reemerged, and the Canadian conversation continued along familiar lines. After the controversial exclusion of Aboriginal issues from the Meech Lake negotiations in 1987, and the failure of the Meech Lake Accord and subsequent trauma of the Oka crisis in 1990, the 1992 Charlottetown Accord included expansive provisions for Aboriginal self-government. These provisions were opposed by the Reform Party and many others on the grounds that they differentiated between Canadians on the basis of race.

Throughout the Charlottetown referendum campaign, many people defended the need for Aboriginal self-government on grounds of justice, often in response to interviewers and commentators who asked questions with a "but isn't difference dangerous?" tone. In one exchange, CBC news anchor Peter Mansbridge asked Ontario attorney general Ian Scott, "I live next door, say, to Elijah Harper. Will he have different rights as a result of this [Charlottetown] agreement than I do? Does he live under a different set of laws?" According to Scott, "The thing to note about Elijah Harper is that for 200 years his people have been living under a regime of different rights and lesser rights than we've had."[41] Those pursuing equal citizenship expressed strong resistance to the self-government provisions on numerous occasions. Gordon Wilson, the leader of the British Columbia Liberal Party, was especially forceful, arguing, "We should have one Canada, indivisible, in which every Canadian is equal to every other Canadian regardless of their race, colour, creed, language, religion, gender or the province in which they live."[42] Historian Michael Bliss, who appeared frequently in the media at the time, asked, "Does our feeling that the Natives of Canada have had a bad deal justify us making this kind of leap, and do we have the faith and the trust necessary, or, are we gonna wake up forty years from now and find out that we've got an order of government based on race, that Aboriginal people are more separate than ever before?"[43]

This equality argument was by far the most common form of opposition put forward by non-Aboriginals to the Aboriginal self-government provisions during the referendum campaign. Interestingly, Bliss utilizes a form of inversion to undermine the differentiated citizenship discourse; by suggesting a connection between Aboriginal self-government, race, and apartheid, he attempts to invert the difference discourse and present it as a hierarchical form of preliberalism.[44] Following the referendum, Mary Ellen Turpel responded to these types of comments, "The equality-for-all argument, coupled with concerns about hierarchies of rights, are, in my view, empty yet troubling strains of opposition to Aboriginal peoples' status and rights in Canadian society. They were powerfully appealing to the public, as suspicion that some Canadians would not be equal to others was effective for the opposition campaign during the referendum debate. These concerns will endure because a discourse was created during the referendum campaign that will be with us for some time to come."[45] As we know, the discourse of equal citizenship was common long before the referendum campaign, but Turpel's fears regarding the enduring strength of the equal citizenship argument are warranted.

Since Charlottetown, a number of important steps have been taken toward achieving forms of Aboriginal self-government. The massive Royal

Commission on Aboriginal Peoples (1991-5), although quickly shelved, called for a new relationship between Aboriginal and non-Aboriginal peoples in Canada. The territory of Nunavut and the Nisga'a Treaty demonstrate the concrete emergence of Aboriginal self-government. Ironically, at the ceremony celebrating the creation of Nunavut, Jean Chrétien said, "That's what's great about Canada. You can be different and be proud of your differences and express them, and at the same time share the advantages and responsibilities of Canadian citizenship. It could not have been expressed in a better way than here."[46] Chief Justice Beverley McLachlin labels this Canadian home space the "Civilization of Difference," which she differentiates from other liberal democratic approaches, especially the unitary American model.[47] And many Canadian scholars, including Alan Cairns, Will Kymlicka, Patrick Macklem, and James Tully, have gained international recognition for their defence of forms of Aboriginal differentiation.[48] This scholarship has considerable appeal on its own terms. Yet I contend that it cannot be understood simply on its own terms. As part of a debate, this literature can be understood only in relation to its debating partners. To illustrate, I return to Alan Cairns.

In 2000, Alan Cairns' *Citizens Plus* was published, as was Tom Flanagan's *First Nations? Second Thoughts*.[49] As the title of his book suggests, Cairns calls for a return to the Hawthorn Report's conception of citizens plus, in contrast to the equal treatment approach taken by Flanagan. The two political scientists have engaged in considerable debate over their respective positions: Cairns depicts Flanagan as taking several steps backward by embracing the logic of the White Paper, and Flanagan does not seem particularly uncomfortable with this charge.[50] Their debate has had wide influence, with extended coverage in the mainstream media – such as the *Globe and Mail* and *National Post* – making specific reference to Cairns and Flanagan and their citizens plus and citizens equal language. With Flanagan currently playing a leading role as advisor to Conservative Party leader Stephen Harper, this debate is likely to remain influential. When one considers all of the changes that have taken place over the last three decades, it is remarkable that these political scientists – like so many other Canadians – are still "here" in the same place, having the same conversation.

The danger is that when presented in the form of a "plus," difference is set within the terms of a hierarchy; difference means more or less than "citizens," which represents the dividing line of equality. Previously, Aboriginal people were "citizens minus" (in the phrase of the Hawthorn Report, i.e., lesser) and now are seen as demanding special rights to be citizens plus (i.e., more). Since all hierarchies are relative, any difference leads to the upgrading or downgrading of those who are merely citizens. Therefore, citizens plus, since it takes the form of more, entails the misrecognition of all other Canadian citizens who are otherwise merely equal (i.e., lesser). Clearly when difference is set within this hierarchical language it cultivates resentment: if "they" get more, "we" get less. With this language, a populist backlash might seem inevitable. Cairns is certainly aware of this problem with the "plus" language, drawing a parallel with similar problems with the language of a distinct society clause for Quebec.[51]

Yet Cairns has other worries too – and here I return to the question he poses in the epigraph of this chapter. Compared with the citizens equal/citizens plus debate of three decades ago, the main difference today is that Aboriginal leaders and intellectuals are less likely to take part. Cairns argues that most of those who defend strong forms of differentiation, whether based on self-government, treaty federalism, or some other mechanism, especially legal scholars, do not pay sufficient attention to the question of how Aboriginal peoples will continue to relate to the whole. According to Cairns, in most discussions of self-government, "Although the saving clause 'within Canada,' is typically noted, relations with Canada are often described in instrumental terms. A pan-Canadian community engaged in common tasks, a coast-to-coast shared citizenship which knits us together in one of our dimensions as a single political people exists at best as a shadowy background reality with little substance. In much of this literature there is a deep, if implicit strain of separatism."[52] "Citizens plus" always had the purpose of integrating Aboriginal peoples *into* Canadian citizenship. And this is where we return to that tension in the Hawthorn Report that I discussed above: in its Hawthorn Report version, the "plus" was a tool to be used by federal bureaucrats in order to facilitate the integration of Aboriginal peoples into the Canadian political community.

The main difference with the contemporary version of the "plus," as it is put forward by Cairns and embraced by others, is that it now presumes democratic governance. As such, the "plus" manner in which Aboriginal people would relate to the Canadian political community would not be determined from above, by non-Aboriginals. In other words, unlike the proposals of the Hawthorn Report, there would be no mechanisms in place ensuring political cohesion by encouraging integration. While Cairns endorses democratic governance, his concern with unity is now magnified. For the Canadian conversation to "succeed," minority and marginalized groups must remain within its orbit. Yet we should not be surprised that Aboriginal leaders and intellectuals are not driven by questions of Canadian unity. Unity questions usually presuppose a majoritarian vantage point, where a minority group is seen as a problem for unity. It is often *because* of the minority group that unity is in question, which is why unity is not in question for the minority group itself.

After all, how can a group be a threat to its own conception of the broader community? In contrast, as soon as we think in terms of *relationships* (e.g., nation-to-nation) there is no longer any fixed reference point, no single vantage point from which to look upon the whole. This is what makes Cairns so uneasy.

In rejecting the unity question, contemporary Aboriginal leaders are not necessarily embracing separatism. Instead, they are coming to realize the sort of paralyzing polarization cultivated by asking the unity question. And they are rejecting ongoing attempts to force Aboriginal people to define themselves vis-à-vis the majoritarian conception of the Canadian political community. Most of all, they are rejecting the logic of thinking of differences in terms of a liberal citizenship arithmetic – of minuses, equals, and pluses, of special or not special, of distinct or not distinct, of more or less.

chapter seven

Misrepresenting the Canadian Conversation

Indifference passes through the wind, the wind that reigns and you breathe, breathe a new passion of inaction, the inaction of politicians, the art of avoiding issues. The issues of culture, the culture of exclusion, the exclusion of the political and the powerlessness. BONG BONG, BONG BONG, BONG BONG; somewhere in this our country, in our government chambers, a watershed of in delight, of muted niceties, unctuous, CLICK, CLICK, CLICK, CLICK, CLICK, CLICK, CLICK, CLICK, CLICK, CLICK ... My vote is a vote of courage. It's a "NO" vote ... It's a vote of no confidence in the process, and no confidence in the political leadership of this country. Being a black person in Canada, being an artist, and being part of the group or groupings that have traditionally been excluded from power, there was some kind of hope that with a kind of knowledge that we have, and the kind of strides that we have been making, that more and more people would be brought to the table, that the whole process will be inclusive, that the constitution will at least acknowledge the realities and the aspirations of various communities. After Meech Lake, we were promised an open process. We were told that things would not be done in the same old way. Well, a process started, and at some point it was closed off.
— Lillian Allen, performed on "My Vote," CBC, 1992

Not all types of politics have a civilizing and binding effect. The type of practice that can hold together diversities and civilize our interaction has certain ground rules. In other words, engaging in a "civilizing" politics does involve a commitment to fundamentals. But it represents acceptance of certain procedural rules regulating the practice rather than agreement about substantive political visions.
— Simone Chambers, "New Constitutionalism: Democracy, Habermas, and Canadian Exceptionalism"

Misrepresenting the Canadian Conversation

As discussed in Chapter 2, those who embrace the Canadian conversation argue that its success lies partly in its very continuation. That is, the conversation succeeds even in the absence of formal agreement – as long as it continues to pursue one. What matters, additionally, is the character of the deliberations themselves. For Simone Chambers, the Canadian conversation does more than succeed; because of its openness to diversity, it is a model for the new constitutionalism. Chambers points to the 1992 Charlottetown referendum campaign as a key example. The Charlottetown campaign is often characterized as representing a significant departure from the much-criticized elitism and exclusivity of the patriation and Meech Lake processes of the 1980s. Widespread consultations preceded the formal negotiations, and there was a referendum process with a vigorous public debate.

Partly as a consequence, scholars have come to celebrate the inclusivity of the Canadian conversation. For example, according to Chambers, "Canadian citizens expect – and are often not disappointed in their expectation – that their claims will be heard and addressed. The darkest moments of Canadian unity have been when one group or another has felt that its claims were not being addressed in the conversation."[1] Similarly, Michael Ignatieff writes, "What makes the Canadian political story so interesting has been the way in which women's organizations, aboriginal groups, and ordinary citizens have forced their way to the table and enlarged both the process of constitutional change and its results."[2] But on what grounds do participants gain access to the Canadian conversation? And to what effects? Since the Canadian conversation is constitutive of the Canadian political community, the nationalist and identitarian struggles that drive it forward do so at procedural as well as substantive levels, especially where questions regarding inclusion and exclusion, impartiality and partiality, are concerned.

In this chapter, I explore the dynamics of the debates that took place during the Charlottetown referendum campaign. During the campaign, there was considerable attention to questions of inclusivity and representation. Procedural discussions of these matters themselves, however, unfolded in ways that cultivated a number of dilemmas for those struggling for better representation. The case of women's groups' efforts to participate in the Charlottetown debate offers a window into how the process of the Canadian conversation itself contributes to "civilizing" difference. In this way, the dynamics and processes of deliberative democracy set up yet another norm against which those who are marginalized are judged. Participation has a "civilizing" effect, as marginalized actors, in this case, women's groups, to justify their presence and demonstrate that they are "good enough" democratic citizens, that they strengthen, rather than challenge, the political community.

Gender Parity

Because there was so much debate over gender inclusion and representation throughout the campaign, one might logically expect it to have centred on the gender parity provision in the accord. Section 23(2) of the draft Charlottetown Accord stated that "the legislature of any province or the legislative authority of any territory may provide for .... any special measures to provide for equal representation of male and female persons."[3] This section would have enabled premiers and territorial leaders to institute rules guaranteeing gender parity for their province or territory in a revised Senate. Four provincial governments, Ontario, Nova Scotia, Saskatchewan, and British Columbia, expressed interest in instituting such measures before the referendum campaign began. Interestingly, although there was some prereferendum campaign debate on this issue, it was brought up only sporadically once the campaign began. Nevertheless, to the extent that it was discussed at all, the media characterized the gender-parity provision as having been thoroughly rejected by the public. For example, when Premier Mike Harcourt suggested that BC adopt the gender-parity model, the CTV reported that the comment "brought a storm of protest," and the CBC noted that "criticism was swift and strong, and the premier appeared to back off the Senate plan."[4]

One of the few major discussions on gender parity in the Senate during the referendum campaign took place between Senator Pat Carney and Alexa McDonough, then leader of the Nova Scotia NDP. Carney rejected the provision: "I don't like it because I find the whole idea of quotas is repugnant to me. A quota system for women confines women, restricts women. It ensures that people think that women couldn't get there on their own and, you know, I've served as a member of Parliament in the House of Commons. It never occurred to me that I was the woman MP or that, even sitting in the Senate, that I'm the woman senator." In response, McDonough pointed out that "surely what's unfair to women is to continue to have them severely underrepresented .... There is a way to ensure that every voter has not one choice, not no choice, but actually two choices. They'll get to vote on two ballots. There'll be a ballot with the male candidate running, a ballot with the female candidate running."[5]

Throughout the campaign, many women attacked the gender-parity provisions and few were heard defending them. One exception was Lillian Allen, the dub poet whose words opened this chapter. She stated, "If we're reforming the Senate ... why don't we do it properly? Why don't we do it right? Why don't we ensure representation of women? Why don't we ensure representation that will reflect the diversity of Canadian society? Why don't we include people from the various communities, the black communities, the Asian communities, and all the people that have been presenting their views? The document is based on exclusion and the time has come for us to reject exclusion."[6] Ironically, although there was a great deal of discussion concerning gender and representation in the campaign process, there was far less on the substantive provision contained in the draft accord.

The Limits of Inclusivity at Charlottetown
Following open public consultations, and in contrast to the Meech Lake negotiations among "eleven white men," the Charlottetown Accord was negotiated by the eleven first ministers (still all white middle-aged men, each with a formal constitutional veto), as well as two territorial leaders (one white man and one white woman) and four Aboriginal leaders (three men and one woman), none of whom had a formal constitutional veto. Though this group was hardly a model of inclusivity, Joe Clark, minister of constitutional affairs, was moved to proclaim that the accord was "decided at the most inclusive negotiating table ever in Canadian history."[7] And this seemed to capture the prevailing sentiment.

The referendum campaign itself marked a high point for the Canadian conversation: it was engaged, public, and inclusive of many voices.

There were, however, notable exclusions, as Lillian Allen's dub poetry suggests, and people with disabilities protested their exclusion from the list of groups recognized in the Canada clause. One event in particular marked the early stages of the campaign. As CBC reporter Joe Schlesinger presented it, "In the Commons, where the constitutional accord has for once brought cozy agreement among the three major parties, the first shots of dissent were heard." Viewers then heard a garbled voice trailing off: "Why are the people at this assembly ...?" Schlesinger then went on to state, "Unheeded by MPs, its source ignored by the cameras, the voice from the visitor's gallery protested the exclusion of the rights of the handicapped from the constitutional deal. The man behind the voice, John Feld, who has multiple sclerosis, was quickly hustled out."[8]

Despite the coverage generated by this event, there was little substantive discussion of disability issues, at least by disability activists. Instead, the leaders of the "yes" and "no" campaigns would periodically criticize or defend the omission of disability from the Canada clause. For example, Ontario premier Bob Rae argued, "The Canada Clause that's there ... when you read it in the context of the Charter of Rights, which is, which is now in place, in my view, does not at all take away from the rights of, of disabled people. In fact, when it refers to the individual and collective freedoms of all Canadians, I think quite specifically it's referring to people with disabilities."[9] Apparently, this specific reference was missed by those for whom it mattered most – and they were denied an opportunity to explain why.

Even where it was inclusive, one of the interesting features of the campaign was the way in which issues of inclusion and exclusion were so often focal points of discussion. For example, the inclusion of Aboriginal people was a topic of extensive discussion. Leading up to Charlottetown, Aboriginal leaders held a number of public rallies to gain support for their inclusion in the negotiations.[10] They were included following a vigorous struggle between several key constitutional actors, especially Ontario premier Bob Rae, who supported Aboriginal inclusion, and Constitutional Affairs Minister Joe Clark, who was a vociferous opponent. Ovide Mercredi, grand chief of the Assembly of First Nations, commented, "What surprised me was not our inclusion ultimately, but Joe Clark's passion for our exclusion."[11] Clark, as well as other constitutional actors, argued that increasing the number of negotiators would decrease the chances of reaching an agreement. And Quebec premier Robert Bourassa felt that Aboriginal representation would so diffuse the focus of the negotiations that Quebec's concerns would receive less attention.

Throughout the referendum campaign, the participation of Aboriginal leaders in the negotiations was publicized widely and celebrated by non-Aboriginals, even while it was challenged in certain ways by some groups of Aboriginal people. The most sustained criticism of the negotiation process came from the Native Women's Association of Canada, which protested the exclusion of Aboriginal women from the negotiation process. NWAC pursued legal action in an unsuccessful attempt to halt the referendum. One of NWAC's lawyers, Mary Eberts, described the situation: "They [NWAC] were given a court order August 20th, saying they were entitled to participate, they have been ignored since then by the Federal government, and we say that the violation of their rights continues down to the present day."[12] Meanwhile Mercredi emphasized that, as grand chief of the Assembly of First Nations, he legitimately represented both male *and* female Status Indians: "The Assembly of First Nations represents Indian people, regardless of their gender, men, women, and children, and at the table we represent the interests of all our people ... The Assembly of First Nations as an organization, represents all these people and the women who belong to our societies can participate in that process and that's how we conducted our affairs so far."[13]

NWAC's protest achieved a fair degree of prominence. In contrast, the gender imbalance among all of the negotiators (fifteen men and two women) arose only periodically as an issue in the campaign. This lack of debate over gender representation was a sharp departure from the Meech Lake process, whose all-male negotiations provided a target for women's groups and others.

One rare example of discussion of the underrepresentation of women in the negotiations received a great deal of attention on both networks. Judy Rebick, president of National Action Committee on the Status of Women

(NAC), was asked at a public forum why she was so concerned about whether the Charlottetown Accord protected women's rights. In response, Rebick recounted a discussion she had had with Fisheries Minister John Crosbie: "'Well, you know,' he says, 'we can't have women there representing women, then we'd have to have cripples and coloured people' ... And I told this story as an example of why we don't trust politicians to defend our equality rights." Crosbie rejected the comments as "inaccurate, vicious in their intent." He then went on, "Special interest groups such as those involving crippled people or coloured people or ethnic groups could hardly be expected to be invited to a constitutional conference. The proper people to be there are the people elected to represent all of the public."[14]

For Crosbie, politicians could legitimately and impartially "represent all of the public" since all citizens elect them. The same could not be said of Rebick, who was not elected, at least not in the parliamentary sense. But the struggle of Rebick and other feminist activists largely resulted from the fact that there were not enough women in politics. Institutional structures required to change this situation did not exist, and it was precisely these sorts of structures that Rebick called for.

Aside from exceptions such as this exchange, most of the media commentary on gender representation in the negotiations centred on the "yes" side's emphatic assertion that the process was open and inclusive. Indeed, commentators often pointed to the presence of Aboriginal negotiators to demonstrate this inclusivity, despite the challenge levelled by NWAC.

Difference Dilemmas

According to Simone Chambers, "The push to accommodate diversity, including diversities that have yet to develop, turns the contract into an open-ended conversation into which new voices can enter at any time."[15] In this way, even when the Canadian conversation includes certain groups, the legitimacy of their inclusion can – and often does – become part of the deliberations, even a central part.

One of the remarkable features of the referendum campaign was the prominence of feminist leaders. Judy Rebick was the most frequently heard "no" spokesperson on the television news (appearing more often than Preston Manning of the Reform Party or even Pierre Trudeau) and the fourth most prominent spokesperson overall.[16] Leading up to the referendum campaign, NAC had consulted extensively with its member groups to develop its wide-ranging critique of the accord. In addition, Rebick and other NAC representatives were supported by a network of feminist scholars, intellectuals, and activists from across the country, allowing them to make well-informed contributions throughout the campaign. Yet a great deal of public debate centred on the legitimacy of NAC and the other women's groups. The nature of this debate generated a series of three dilemmas for these participants, which exemplify what legal scholar Martha Minow has called the "dilemma of difference." Given situations of marginalization, it is necessary to resist, to gain inclusion, by poking through the false neutrality that often conceals power imbalances. The process of doing so, however, may reinforce the "difference" in ways that can lead to further marginalization and stigmatization.[17]

Dilemma of Exclusion/Inclusion

NAC, and specifically its claim to represent women's voices in its role as an umbrella organization of women's groups, was criticized as illegitimate because its leadership was not elected by all Canadians. This criticism was doubly ironic given that NAC was itself challenging the legitimacy of an electoral system cultivating the extreme underrepresentation of women. Furthermore, a referendum is a time for public deliberation, in which rules governing the election of parliamentary representatives should not apply to speakers' participation.

Dilemma of Im/partiality

Despite the referendum setting and its orientation to public deliberation, assumptions of representative democracy prevailed insofar as elected representatives (especially federal and provincial) spoke frequently in the media in their *representative voices*. Certainly, aside from politicians, there were also many writers, academics, commentators, and popular "citizen on a street corner"-type voices. The voices most often questioned, however, were those, including the voices of NAC, that emerged out of new social movement processes, the so-called special interests.

In response, some women (especially feminist activists and politicians) pointed to women's underrepresentation and questioned the traditional premise of impartial representation altogether, arguing that men could not possibly speak to their issues, needs, and experiences as women. This type of strategic reversal is crucial, to be sure, but the dilemma is that women (and other traditionally underrepresented and marginalized actors) are further categorized and grouped in the very process of gaining and justifying inclusion, all of which produces a tangle of static either/or frames of analysis.

For example, even though NWAC and its court challenge received sustained coverage, much of this coverage centred on claims that NWAC itself was acting illegitimately in bringing forth its protest, on the basis that it could not speak for all Status Indian women. *CTV News* stated, "There are other Aboriginals who say the Native Women's Association does not speak for the traditional Native women," while on the CBC, Wendy Grant, chief of the

Musqueam Nation, said, "The Native Women's Association, although they have concerns, do not speak on behalf of the traditional women within our societies."[18] It is debatable whether NWAC was ever presuming to speak for all Aboriginal women, or even for all Status Indian women. Rather than stimulating debate over whether the negotiations should have included Aboriginal women, however, NWAC's protest resulted in a struggle over who could legitimately represent Aboriginal women during the referendum campaign.

Where NAC was concerned, the media began giving more attention to other women (mainly conservative politicians and commentators), who emphasized their impartiality by insisting aggressively upon the irrelevance of their gender (or ethnicity, race, etc.) to their roles as politicians or in their decisions as citizens and voters. Numerous reports asking whom NAC spoke for aired throughout the referendum campaign. In virtually every case the media asked women to answer that question, and many prominent women did just that. The common refrain was "NAC doesn't speak for me!"[19] The following CBC report was characteristic of this questioning:

> *Peter Mansbridge:* The "YES" forces in the referendum campaign are reflecting tonight on a setback. The National Action Committee on the Status of Women, a group they'd like to have onside, will instead be an opponent. NAC is voting "NO." The group announced its decision yesterday. But a lot of people wonder just who NAC speaks for, and how much influence it might have in the campaign.
>
> *Kathleen Mahoney:* I don't think it's a bad deal for women. I think it could be better.
>
> *Karen Webb:* Some women, such as law professor and feminist, Kathleen Mahoney, say NAC doesn't speak for them on this issue. She says although the deal could be better, its problems aren't big ones ... It's not clear NAC can deliver the votes of the half-million Canadians it says it represents. It has the organization, but very little money. And many well-known feminists, including those in the major political parties, appear to be lining up on the other side.[20]

In another example, June Callwood, novelist and co-chair of the "Yes" Committee, commented, "I'm somewhat uneasy about all this pressure for gender equality, which deals only with genitalia and not with content. I've known some antifeminist women, lots of them, and I've known some really fine profeminist men. There's something simplistic about thinking that one's gender defines character."[21] As Callwood's unease suggests, it is as if women were presented with the choice of situating their voices in either a disembodied (impartial) manner or an essentialized (partial) manner. Of course, whatever path they "chose," their voices were marked as "women's voices" by virtue of their being faced with the choice. In contrast, speakers from traditionally overrepresented groups were largely immune to such questioning and thus free to express themselves in a fluid manner, emphasizing their partiality on some issues (speaking, say, as "Westerners" or "rural farmers") while assuming an impartial voice (as "Canadian") on others. While expressions of provincial, regional, and language partiality garnered little attention, women participants were, as a whole, constructed as selfishly focused on issues of concern only to them.

Dilemma of Disunity

In their presence as differentiated voices seeking inclusion, and in having to justify their inclusion, the voices of NAC and other feminist or minority actors were thus constructed as partial. These groups were continually criticized for having a fragmenting effect on the Canadian political community, one that threatened the Canadian conversation itself. This is one reason it was so difficult for them to displace the impartial/partial opposition. While NAC received considerable attention in the media, referendum actors often portrayed it as a selfish interest group. In a typical example, Joe Clark stated, "The problem with an interest group is that it focuses so narrowly on its narrow interests, that it can lose sight of the country. In my view, that is what NAC has done here."[22]

Many others put forward similar interpretations during and after the referendum campaign. Economist John Crispo commented during a television interview, "My fear is that too many of us are going to be voting as little Canadians when it comes to the referendum vote. What do I mean by little Canadians? I'm talking about little English Canadians, little French Canadians, little Native Canadians, little new Canadians, little any kind of Canadians ... They see a little bush that represents their vested interests and they're kind of saying, 'What's in this for me or my group,' not what's in it for Canada."[23] Crispo placed great emphasis on the "challenges" that the inclusion of formerly marginalized actors – namely, Aboriginal people, women's groups, and ethnic and racial minorities – presented for Canadian politics.

Gendered Citizens, Good and Bad

This view has been put forward by many others, beyond the Charlottetown campaign itself. For Samuel LaSelva, "What has occurred is a virtual explosion of identities, such that women, gays, ethnics, and Quebec and Aboriginal nationalists vie one against the other."[24] Alan Cairns speaks of struggles over representation in similar terms, noting that while they "do not threaten the survival of the constitutional order, they do challenge the norms of a universal, common citizenship. This is especially evident with respect to the theory and practice of representation and makes increasingly difficult the task of the state, via the politician, of representing, accommodating, and transcending the diversities of Canadian society."[25]

During the Charlottetown campaign, Cairns expressed concern over the plethora of diverse voices being heard in various political arenas. Interests had multiplied to include actors both vocal and particularistic, leaving Canadian citizenship fragmented.

In response to such concerns, Will Kymlicka suggests that a distinction be made between groups pursuing self-government and marginalized groups seeking better representation. In making the distinction, he notes that "whereas demands for representation by disadvantaged groups take the larger political community for granted, and seek greater inclusion within it, demands for self-government reflect a desire to weaken the bonds with the larger community, and indeed question that larger community's very nature, authority and permanence. If democracy is the rule of the people, self-government raises the question of who 'the people' really are."[26]

This distinction is problematic, however, because it measures demands for better representation in terms of whether they strengthen or weaken unity. Furthermore, women and other underrepresented groups are most certainly challenging – in a fundamental way – "who 'the people' really are." The unity criterion is set from above, from the perspective of those who can speak on behalf of the "the people." When women demand inclusion, they are challenging the masculine premise of "we the people."

In response to the critics, Chambers emphasizes the binding, and thus stabilizing, effect that the Canadian conversation can have, such as with deliberations over "special representation." She calls on scholars to examine questions of stability in parallel with questions of justice.[27] Still, there is a danger in conflating the need for greater inclusivity with questions of integration, stability, and unity. A unity framing places the disadvantaged group on display and disciplines the group by way of the expectation that they demonstrate civilized behaviour.

Linda Trimble has also responded to the critics by demonstrating that women participants in the referendum campaign were – despite all of the efforts to construct them as hyper-particularistic – actually "good citizens" who made productive contributions in their own distinctive ways.[28] In making this case, Trimble displaces the impartiality/partiality opposition by arguing that women were other-regarding and concerned for the whole. Unfortunately, however, she substitutes a new opposition when she adopts a "good citizen" (looking out for the whole) framing, which implies a contrast with a "bad citizen" (challenging the whole). Why operate within this opposition?

Trimble's response illustrates further the sorts of dilemmas – following from the dilemma of difference – that the Canadian conversation generates for those struggling for inclusion. In questioning their underrepresentation, women are themselves questioned as illegitimate and unrepresentative. In the process, they are further grouped as different, as driven by a partial perspective, as undermining the attempts of the Canadian conversation to constitute a people, and so on. Trimble rejects this characterization, arguing that women were in fact acting as "good citizens," directed at strengthening the political community in their own distinctive ways. I have no disagreement with Trimble on this point, but what is most important about her argument is that she is moved to make it.

Is it possible that this type of response by those struggling for inclusion is what Chambers means when she speaks of the potential civilizing effects of the Canadian conversation? In participating in this terrain, women and other traditionally underrepresented groups are conditioned to engage in these civilizing processes, which orient them toward diffusing the threat that their *own* participation may represent for the constitution of the political community. Rebick and NAC are not easily "civilized," to be sure. In fact, Rebick was the Charlottetown referendum's prototypical *bad* citizen in her sustained pursuit of a transformative politics, which moved well beyond questions of underrepresentation to challenge prevailing definitions of "the people" and the gender order itself. Other participants in the Canadian conversation constructed NAC as threatening because it *was*. Because of its "uncivilized" behaviour (i.e., NAC's opposition to the accord), the federal government cut back NAC's funding sharply following the referendum.

For those wishing to pursue a transformative politics, "bad" citizenship remains the preferred option, yet who would want to choose between these dichotomous options in the first place? As many Canadians continue to struggle for gender parity, with electoral reform increasingly on the agenda, it makes sense to steer clear of the Canadian conversation, in which questions of gender justice are so quickly supplanted by depoliticizing concerns over unity and stability.

chapter eight

Civil Eyes:
Seeing "Difference Blind"

> The government will promote creative encounters and interchange among all Canadian cultural groups in the interest of national unity.
> – Pierre Trudeau, "Statement on Multiculturalism,"
> House of Commons, 8 October 1971

> Liberalism can't and shouldn't claim complete cultural neutrality. Liberalism is also a fighting creed. The hospitable variant I espouse, as well as the most rigid forms, has to draw the line.
> – Charles Taylor, "The Politics of Recognition"

A few years ago, while walking through the campus of McMaster University, I came upon a student sitting behind a table publicizing a "Diversity Lunch" as part of "Unity Week" at the university. I have always found the juxtaposition of diversity and unity interesting and so I asked the student why they had called it "Unity Week." She answered, "We decided to do more than just race, so we called it 'Unity Week.'" I asked her to expand on this and she said, "It's about unity because we are uniting diverse people ... In Canada, we are very diverse – but we should still be united." I pressed on: "Why the 'but'? Why do we need a 'but' after the phrase 'in Canada, we are very diverse'?" The reason, the student explained, is "because we are not united – diversity scares people."[1]

In this familiar way, Canadian celebrations of diversity are often followed by a "but" clause, as if to neutralize diversity's dangers. To provide another illustration, at a workshop entitled "The 'Canadian' Diversity Model," hosted by the Canadian Policy Research Network, one of the participants, after making his support of diversity clear, was moved to add, "but this does not mean that anything goes; we are not returning to the state of nature here."[2] Similarly, in the epigraph above, while Charles Taylor depicts his communitarian liberalism as more "hospitable" to diversity, it still "has to draw the line" somewhere.

Canadian "nations," as imagining communities, take shape through such line-drawing contests. With so many complex and overlapping internal and external boundaries up for discussion, the Canadian conversation continues in pursuit of some form of agreement. How much differentiation, how much group recognition, how many group rights? The Canadian conversation polarizes over these questions because the character and placement of the limits pursued by the nationalisms corresponds to their own conception of the Canadian political community. These are confounding debates; a great deal is on the line when Canadians try to agree on where to draw the line.

These struggles over the character and placement of the limit are intertwined with recognition struggles. This is where the "diversity lunch" and similar diversity practices come into play. As commonplace as such practices have become in Canada, it was not so long ago that scholars of "consociational democracy" argued that intergroup conflict was best managed through elite accommodation: the less interaction between groups of people across their differences, the better.[3] It is doubtful whether consociational democracy was ever reflected in Canadian practice, yet Canadian diversity governance now follows an altogether different model, along the lines that Trudeau proposed back in 1971. Rather than keeping citizens apart, Canadians are encouraged to interact, to learn about one another, across their differences.

In this chapter, I explore the relationship between the line-drawing contests of the Canadian conversation, their relationship to the politics of recognition, and their mediation through forms of multicultural interaction. Drawing from Michel Foucault's work on panopticism and governmentality, I analyze a peculiar form of liberal governmentality directed at managing Canada's diverse population. Paradoxically, the citizen interaction that results from what I call multicultural panopticism is a basis for cohesion, even as it aims to define and differentiate.

Still, while multicultural study is driven to recognize the identities of Canadians, it is just as likely to misrecognize them as somehow beyond the limit of liberalism, leading to a continuous succession of mis/recognition struggles. For the misrecognized group, multicultural study provides multiple opportunities to correct distorted representations. In seeking to be recognized more accurately and appropriately, the misrecognized group places its liberalism on display, with civilizing effects.

Kymlicka, Unity, and the Discourse of the Limit
In Chapters 2 through 7, I analyzed the nationalist and identitarian contestation surrounding attempts to shape, reshape, and indeed extend the limits of Canadian liberalism to include forms of differentiated and asymmetrical categories. Over the last decade, numerous political theorists have made the

case for multiculturalism within liberal principles of justice. According to Kymlicka's well-known formulation, on the one hand, liberals should reject the many forms of external restriction frequently imposed on minorities. On the other hand, liberals must also reject situations wherein minority groups impose restrictions on their individual members. For Kymlicka, such internal restrictions are beyond the limit of what a liberal democratic society should tolerate in the practices of its minority populations.[4]

The character and location of the limit continues to preoccupy liberal theorists,[5] even though Kymlicka argues that the normative philosophical debate over liberal justice and minority rights is "drawing to a close" (with the theorists of differentiated citizenship victorious) and that the debate has shifted toward issues of unity and integration.[6] Yet I suggest that in the Canadian context, the debate over multiculturalism has never left this unity problematic. Nor has it left the debate over minority rights and the limit.

Where the unity problematic is concerned, the Canadian multiculturalism policy emerged in the late 1960s and early 1970s, following the Royal Commission on Bilingualism and Biculturalism. The original mandate of the commission to examine biculturalism was rejected by so-called "other ethnic groups" in favour of what eventually became multiculturalism. Trudeau embraced this shift as part of his unity strategy, unveiling Canada's (and the world's) first multiculturalism policy in 1971, stating that "although there are two official languages, there is no official culture, nor does any ethnic group take precedence over any other."[7] As many have argued, Trudeau feared that a bicultural understanding of Canada would sharpen Canadian dualism and encourage Québécois nationalism, so he pursued multiculturalism instead, thereby accentuating Canadian cultural diversity more generally. It is not surprising, then, that the policy has always been regarded with suspicion in Quebec, even as most of its principles are pursued there.

In English Canada, Reginald Bibby, Neil Bissoondath, Richard Gwyn, and many others, criticize multiculturalism for encouraging division and fragmentation: the familiar argument is that it "ghettoizes" ethnic groups in particularistic communities, weakening the bonds that hold Canadians together and cultivating a disruptive and divisive identity politics.[8] As a unity policy aimed at combating Canadian dualism, it is ironic that it is now charged with divisiveness. However, supporters of the policy have met the criticism squarely; in particular, Will Kymlicka argues that the policy manages tensions and has an integrationist effect, thereby enhancing cohesion and unity.

In this way, debate over the policy (including the original 1971 policy and the subsequent Multiculturalism Act, 1988) is often dichotomous. The trigger points – around the recognition of some form of diversity – route a variety of otherwise distinctive emancipatory concerns over race, ethnicity, culture, and religion into debates over the character of the Canadian political community. Should racial, ethnic, and cultural minorities receive distinct recognition and support to preserve and develop their diverse backgrounds? Should school curricula reflect diverse traditions and histories? Should the uniforms and headgear of Mounties allow for religious diversity? Are affirmative action and employment equity programs justified? As these questions over justice, equality, and diversity are incorporated into the Canadian conversation, they are approached as problems (or solutions) for the whole, leading the discussion to polarize: hyphenated versus unhyphenated citizenship, liberalism versus communitarianism, "difference-blind" versus difference liberalism, and so on. The critics and supporters of multiculturalism and related policies present diametrically opposed interpretations of their effects. They agree implicitly, however, on the criterion of judgment: does it appropriately manage the challenge of diversity and does it enhance or weaken Canadian unity?

Where the minority rights problematic is concerned, Kymlicka is well aware of the misrecognition that results from the liberal discourse of the limit. Yet he also worries about the anxieties generated by the presence of the potentially illiberal other. For example, he points to Neil Bissoondath, who notes, "Because we have failed to establish the limits of diversity, because we have so blithely accepted the mentality of division, we find ourselves lost in a confusion of values. Multiculturalism has made us fearful of defining acceptable boundaries; it has caused us to confuse the establishment of circumscription with a lack of respect. And so we find ourselves in danger of accepting, in its name, a slide into ethical chaos."[9] Kymlicka emphasizes that Bissoondath and other critics of the Canadian multiculturalism policy such as Richard Gwyn are right to express concern over the limit. Kymlcka believes that while such concerns are well intentioned, these critics fail to observe that the limit is in fact already firmly in place. His scholarly task is to correct this oversight by demonstrating the presence of the limit in Canadian multiculturalism policy and the Charter of Rights and Freedoms; he calls upon the Canadian government to emphasize and publicize the existence of the limit in its diversity-related policies and practices.

But why do these well-intentioned critics of multiculturalism so frequently misinterpret the policy as failing to impose limits? A lack of information about the policy is unlikely to be the reason. To try to set the record straight with empirical evidence, as Kymlicka does, is to misunderstand the purpose of the discourse of the limit; in its public manifestations, its purpose is to construct the boundaries of the Canadian political community. Kymlicka wishes to put these Canadians at ease, and it is notable that he does so by catering to their nationalist concerns: "What many Canadians really worry about is the future of multiculturalism – in particular, whether it has put us on a slippery slope leading away from social and political integration and towards acceptance of any form of 'cultural difference,' regardless of its impact on Canadian institutions and principles."[10]

By framing multiculturalism in this way, Kymlicka conflates "cultural difference," at least in its potential, with practices that threaten Canadian "social and political integration" and "Canadian institutions and principles." Canadians need to know that multiculturalism does not allow "any form of 'cultural difference,'" but only ones that do not threaten the character of Canada in these ways.

A logic of identity is in effect here, for the discourse of the limit is premised on a reified understanding of diversity. Minority groups are constructed by Kymlicka as if they have certain authentic ways of being based on tradition, custom, or culture, which they are driven to actualize when given the opportunity. Multiculturalism is designed to provide minority groups with just such an opportunity, but only to a point. In other words, the minority group is free to practise its authentic traditions, except where they are illiberal, where they contravene the rule of law or other basic principles of a liberal democratic society. The minority group is constructed in overly homogeneous terms, as if its practices were not themselves always contested and reflective of power relations. If a minority group member behaves illiberally, it is because he or she is actualizing certain customs or behaviours that define the identity of the group as a whole.

The discourse of the limit acts like a safety net for Canadians, so that they can celebrate diversity – despite its dangers – knowing that there is a limit to minority behaviours that threaten to move beyond what is deemed acceptable. It constructs "Canadians" as not only liberal but also as the guardians of liberal values in the face of the illiberal potential of the other. The continual strenuous assertion of the limit implies a latent desire on the part of the minority to behave illiberally, generating multiple cases of misrecognition.

Taylor's Politics of Recognition

One of Taylor's central arguments in his essay "The Politics of Recognition" is that the politics of difference often involves demands for group recognition. Thus Quebec demands to be recognized as a distinct society. Taylor holds that such demands are rooted in the idea that our identities are formed by recognition and, as a result, misrecognition must be considered a harm.[11] Taylor distinguishes between moderate demands for recognition of the sort pursued by Quebec and Aboriginal people, which he defends, and other more extreme demands that he believes are unjustified. Moderate demands for recognition take the form of a presumption that "all human cultures that have animated whole societies over some considerable stretch of time have something important to say to all human beings."[12] The problem with many defenders of the canon is that they seem to suggest that the cultural output of non-European societies is likely to be inferior or unworthy. Taylor argues that this assessment can only be rooted in Eurocentric prejudice and an intolerable sense of superiority. This leads him to endorse a moderate presumption of equal respect for all cultures. Yet Taylor is troubled by a more extreme demand that "we all *recognize* the equal value of different cultures; that we not only let them survive, but acknowledge their *worth*."[13]

For Taylor, the alternative to simply granting positive judgments whenever they are sought is to undertake serious study of the other cultures. He argues that the presumption of equal worth requires "not peremptory and inauthentic judgments of equal value, but a willingness to be open to comparative cultural study of the kind that must displace our horizons in the resulting fusions. What it requires above all is an admission that we are very far away from that ultimate horizon from which the relative worth of different cultures might be evident."[14]

Taylor is well aware of the problems of interpretation that intercultural study involves. We bring to it a range of particularistic interpretive assumptions, including those related to cultural worth, which may distort our judgment. He draws from Gadamer's notion of a "fusion of horizons" so that, instead of simply importing criteria of value specific to our own culture, we enter into a broader horizon where these criteria may be placed alongside other criteria, such as those specific to the culture being studied. The resulting fusion of horizons transforms us, Taylor believes, fostering the development of more sensitive vocabularies of comparison and contrast, so that we do not merely judge the Other using our old, unexamined standards and criteria. As a result, we will be able to advance a respectful and appropriate form of mutual understanding and recognition.

Taylor's main premise is that groups demanding recognition have an authentic basis, inhabit a definable cultural space, within which they may be studied and judged. Even though Taylor emphasizes that identities are formed dialogically, he understands this formation in terms of one coherent identity group's constructing itself in relation to another. Taylor excludes from the politics of recognition identity categories that are not unified and coherent: "The claim is that all human cultures that have animated whole societies over some *considerable stretch of time* have something important to say to all human beings. I have worded it in this way to *exclude partial cultural milieux* within a society, as well as *short phases* of a major culture."[15] Thus, Taylor explicitly excludes, by definition, many minority cultures as well as hybrid identities from his politics of recognition.[16]

I do not wish to dispute Taylor's claim that identities are formed in important respects by processes of recognition or that misrecognition constitutes a harm. Furthermore, I agree with Taylor that the facile granting of recognition often involves an unbearably patronizing stance. Finally, if judgment of the other were in fact *necessary,* as Taylor suggests, then it seems to me that on a pragmatic level Gadamer's fusion of horizons is a far better ideal than the various monological alternatives, however difficult or impossible to achieve in practice.[17] Still, Taylor's overarching premise merits further attention: namely, the premise that we must study one another across our differences.

The notion of a fusion of horizons makes many people uncomfortable, of course, because it is no longer evident who is in a position to monitor ethical boundaries and on what bases. As Homi Bhabha notes, "Liberal discourses on multiculturalism ... anxiously acknowledge the attenuation in the authority of the Ideal Observer, an authority that oversees the ethical rights (and insights) of the liberal perspective from the top deck of the Clapham omnibus."[18] There is now further anxiety over whether the limits are being properly monitored.

Multicultural Panopticism: From Surveillance to Coveillance

Canadians view one another through a taxonomic lens and they often express pride in the diverse patterns they see, since they believe that it is part of what makes the country distinctive. In the inclusive and liberal spirit of the multicultural mosaic, Canadians celebrate the vitality of the country's many ethnic, cultural, religious, or "lifestyle" communities. One may be inclined to interpret this as a sign of considerable toleration, yet Canadians do not simply put up with their diversity as the word toleration would suggest; their approach to diversity is actively, and even insistently, forward and enthusiastic.

There is something peculiar about this spirited display of diversity. At times, it is as if Canada's diverse groups are not simply *allowed* to exist and express themselves, they are *expected* to do so, to place themselves on public display. Much as Trudeau proposed when unveiling the multiculturalism policy in 1971, there is an epistemic régime in operation here, directed at the collection and presentation of diversity-related knowledge.[19] I now turn to analyze these practices, drawing from Michel Foucault's work on panopticism and governmentality.

The panopticon originated in the late eighteenth century in the writings of the utilitarian reformer Jeremy Bentham. In *Discipline and Punish,* Foucault presents Bentham's panopticon as a central technique in what was at the time an emerging form of disciplinary power.[20] Bentham designed the panopticon as a prison with a very peculiar architecture: the building was circular, like a ring surrounding a central guard tower; the prison cells were located around the ring and were completely open to the disciplinary gaze of the guards, putting the prisoners under constant surveillance; furthermore, the guard tower was designed so the prisoners could not see inside and, as a result, would never know when the guard was actually watching. The gaze turns inward and the prisoners begin to monitor themselves, making the panopticon a remarkably efficient disciplinary mechanism. As Foucault states, "Thanks to its mechanisms of observation, it gains in efficiency and in the ability to penetrate into men's behaviour."[21] The disciplinary gaze is not only efficient but produces and constructs as it analyzes, categorizes, and differentiates the characteristics and behaviours of the prisoners.

For Foucault, panopticism functions as a more general technique of governance, and it is in this sense that I speak of multicultural panopticism.[22] Multicultural panopticism alters the architectural design, however, by levelling the guard tower. This changes the mechanisms of surveillance, for there is no longer any single place of observation; there are no "guards" nor are there any "prisoners." Instead, multicultural panopticism replaces the guards with multicultural citizens. Distinct from the practice of surveillance, multicultural panopticism operates through a more fluid "coveillance," a term used by Steven Mann, Jason Nolan, and Barry Wellman to describe "observation that is side-to-side ... which could include one citizen watching another,"[23] as in a neighbourhood. According to these authors, in "a coveillance society, the actions of all may, in theory, be observable and accountable to all."[24]

Instead of prisoners, then, multicultural panopticism has multicultural citizens who are not only "free" but also encouraged to express their freedom through multicultural coveillance. Whereas the prisoners cannot see one another, multicultural coveillance assumes participatory citizens who see and are seen. This is a form of diversity governance.

Foucault began examining the "art of government" in the late 1970s, analyzing the ways in which populations are governed.[25] There is a great deal of scholarly commentary on this period of Foucault's work, which I draw from in what follows.[26] Governmentality operates somewhere between Foucault's earlier notion of power and the more traditional concept of domination. Foucault describes its operation: "We must distinguish the relationship of power as strategic games between liberties – strategic games that result in the fact that some people try to determine the conduct of others – and the states of domination, which are what we ordinarily call power. And, between the two, between the games of power and the states of domination, you have governmental technologies."[27]

In contrast to traditional ways of understanding power and domination, of one group *over* another, Foucault's notion of power works *through* the freedom of others. Foucault's concept of governmentality, then, occupies the spaces between power and domination. Governmentality involves the "conduct of conduct," or the rational application of techniques designed to regulate people and their actions: it involves directing individuals, groups, and populations to regulate their own behaviour and the behaviour of others.

Foucault argues that in modern times government has become less focused on maintaining sovereignty and more concerned with the conduct of populations. As he says, "population comes to appear above all else as the ultimate end of government. In contrast to sovereignty, government has as its purpose not the act of government itself, but the welfare of the population, the improvement of its condition."[28] Foucault does not present governmentality as limited to the regulating actions of governments or states;[29] instead, the term should be considered in a wider sense to include all institutions, practices, and techniques that operate on a population. In presenting his notion of governmentality, Foucault does not privilege the typical distinction between state and non-state institutions and practices; in this way, he contrasts sharply with traditions of political theory that emphasize questions of consent, legitimacy, and the sovereignty of the state.[30]

Foucault differentiates between a number of different manifestations of governmentality. I am concerned in particular with his understanding of the liberal form. While some scholars cast doubt on the possibility of agency in Foucault's theorizing, Foucault theorizes power as operating *through* the behaviour of free subjects. As Gordon puts it, Foucault believes that "power is defined as actions on others' actions: that is, it presupposes rather than annuls their capacity as agents; it acts upon, and through, an open set of practical and ethical possibilities."[31] Despite this, Foucault believes that liberal governmentality rests on a serious tension. On the one hand, since it presumes "free" liberal subjects, it must itself be a restrained form of government; since it involves a critique of power, it must be a reflective form of government. On the other hand, liberal governance must be powerful enough to ensure that the freedom of its subjects is properly secured. As a result of this tension, Foucault suggests that freedom itself becomes the focus of management. In particular, it is necessary to secure the sorts of conditions likely to induce liberal subjects to express their freedom in certain ways, and this often involves a training or regulation of these subjects. Liberal governance must operate on and through the freedom of individuals since, as Barry Hindess puts it, "members of the relevant population cannot always be expected to have developed the thought and behaviour habits of 'free' and 'independent' persons."[32]

The tension within liberal governmentality parallels a tension inherent in the Canadian case. Here, the conduct of the Canadian population – as a *diverse* population – is the object of pervasive governmental scrutiny because diversity generates considerable cultural anxiety and thus represents a problem that must be acted upon to ensure cohesion and stability. Yet multicultural governance, as a distinctly liberal strategy, is subject to important limitations since it must take seriously the freedom of the subject. Rather than suppress diversity, then, multicultural governance acts *through* the multicultural subject, to facilitate the playing out of diversity along certain less threatening paths. Diversity is not simply allowed to thrive; it is encouraged to do so – *taught* to do so.

How does multicultural panopticism operate? Just as the object of liberal governance is the construction of the normalized liberal subject, multicultural governance has the purpose of constructing normalized multicultural citizens within a taxonomic régime of identity and diversity. Multicultural governance does far more than protect the spaces within which diversity can flourish; it helps to create these spaces. While multiculturalism may seem to illustrate the functioning of a kind of negative cultural freedom (i.e., freedom from state intrusion), multicultural governance constructs the identity framework within which this freedom may play out, operating on the population so that the spaces of diversity are in fact occupied and ensuring that freedom is expressed in an appropriate manner.

Canadians cannot know a priori how to express themselves in multicultural terms, but must instead be trained to understand, and operate within, the categorization process of multicultural citizenship. The multicultural gaze is directed at an individual and says, in effect, this is who you are (i.e., Ukrainian, Korean, Jamaican, gay, disabled). Canadians are "hailed" or called into their identity categories as if to say, *you are this and she is that, and this is how we differentiate between people.*[33]

Multicultural panopticism encourages certain types of citizen interactions by providing the categories and differences within which individuals and groups of citizens can negotiate their behaviour and their relations with others. Multicultural citizenship is normalized as Canadians participate in the practice of coveillance. This is not unlike the model proposed by Parekh: "Properly understood and freed from the polemical exaggerations of its advocates and detractors, multicultural education is an education in freedom, both in the sense of freedom *from* prejudices and biases and freedom *to* explore and learn from other cultures and perspectives."[34] While multicultural coveillance particularizes citizens into their various categories, the common act of placing one's diversity on display constructs and reinforces a more general basis for cohesion and unity. Multicultural panopticism is normalized as an ethically superior form of political interaction.

One example that encapsulates the character of multicultural panopticism rather nicely is the Canadian Broadcasting Corporation television program

Culture Shock, described on its web page as follows: "This show is about discovery. Discovering the true personality of a neighbour you barely know after 200 years. This show is about exploration. Exploring the lifestyle and the values that make up Canada's cultural diversity. A group of bilingual young Canadians, from all regions of Canada, trade places and experience the reality of living in a different milieu, using a different language ... Tune in to *Culture Shock* and discover a cultural reality you knew little about." The *Culture Shock* website also includes a number of episode descriptions:

> *Who are the real Indians?* A new immigrant from India, Sachin Deshpande travels to Manitoulin Island in Ontario where he attends an aboriginal pow-wow. Sachin tries to figure out who are the real Indians ... He compares native customs with the spiritual beliefs of his own country.
>
> *A true culture shock:* A young reporter of South Asian origin, Shachi Kurl leaves her multicultural Vancouver to immerse herself in the francophone culture of the Saguenay-Lac-Saint Jean. For the first time in her life she is exposed to a society that is culturally and linguistically homogeneous.
>
> *Gay World:* Nicolas Desrosiers explores the reality of living in the gay world. Now that the gay lifestyle is widely acknowledged by marketing firms and the political apparatus, Nicolas wondered if everything was rosy in the gay world.[35]

Notable here is that in addition to learning the importance of identity-display, these Canadians are expected to recognize these displays in others.

Seeing "Difference Blind"

The multicultural panopticism I have depicted herein may well enhance mutual understanding and respect. It is, for the most part, an inclusionary practice directed at cultivating harmony and cohesion. At its most "comfortable," multicultural panopticism may take on an ironic tone, celebrating hybridity and postmodern pastiche. Still, it is hypersensitive to danger. Premised on the potential of the Other to move "beyond the limit," it can shift quickly into policing mode as certain groups begin to get "unruly." Because Canada is a self-consciously multicultural community, however, the exclusionary logic of the Canadian discourse of the limit is itself subject to limits. A minority group cannot be excluded, at least not without contradiction, simply because it is considered too different or too exotic as that would conflict with the central premise of multiculturalism itself, which aims to be open, inclusive, and welcoming to diversity. Canada's problem of diversity, upon which the discourse of the limit is premised, must be presented as a problem of diversity becoming illiberal since other "problems" of diversity contradict the inclusive logic of multiculturalism.

Not all Canadians are "hailed" in the same manner or to the same extent: the multicultural gaze centres on the margins. The mainstream is only rarely on display or rather, the mainstream is always on display but only rarely in the form of problematized identity categories. The politics of the discourse of the limit – as a part of the Canadian conversation – generates misrecognition but also provides a civilizing space for recognition to be pursued and granted. Forms of resistance that operate through the politics of recognition often serve to reinforce the ways in which those who are marginalized are defined, categorized, and normalized.

To return to Taylor's understanding of misrecognition: the Other is hailed as in some respects inferior, as an example of a less developed cultural form. Taylor rightly understands this to be a type of harm and so he defends and justifies the subsequent demand for recognition. Yet this demand for recognition, as an attempt to resist the process of misrecognition, has paradoxical effects. The typical response to misrecognition takes the following form: *We are not how you describe us* [i.e., illiberal, less civilized, criminals, etc.]; *quite the contrary, we are* [an important and contributing group in society with such and such characteristics and values] *and we demand to be recognized as such.* Even when the results are "successful," the dialogue of misrecognition and recognition effectively defines the group in question in relation to the liberal limit, displaying its characteristics and essential qualities. Whether a group is recognized or misrecognized, it is always defined so that even resistance to misrecognition reinforces the logic of identity on which the original misrecognition was itself based. The gaze may take on a positive shine, but the gaze remains. I would take this even further: recognition can be freely granted at least partly because the truth value of the judgment is rarely the only issue under contestation, if it is contested at all. When a marginalized group sees a distorted and demeaning image of itself depicted by the dominant culture, it tries to become empowered by replacing that image, but the process of categorization and knowledge construction proceeds apace. Even while identities are fluid, overlapping, and internally diverse, they are in important respects constructed and reconstructed in essentialist terms through the demand for recognition.

Furthermore, misrecognition cannot be understood outside relations of power and domination. It is the misrecognized group that reinforces its "groupness" in the attempt to gain recognition. A group marked out as inferior or of lower status attempts to achieve equality by struggling for a more positive marking. Yet in either case, the group is marked and the process of resistance serves to reinforce the marking, to reinforce the group as a totality. Dominant groups are not, by definition, misrecognized in this way, and thus do not need to have the lens of multicultural study focused on them. They are far less likely to be cast in totalizing categories and so they have greater freedom to pursue overlapping and hybrid identities.

(Mis)recognition is dispensed in an arbitrary manner, but the main issue is not whether a particular group deserves or does not deserve recognition. The main issue is that the group actually seeks recognition, for in order to seek recognition, a group must become integrated into the taxonomic terrain of multicultural panopticism.

chapter nine

There's No Place Like Home

> Nationalism is not a "force" to be measured as resurgent or receding. It is a heterogeneous set of "nation"-oriented idioms, practices, and possibilities that are continuously available or "endemic" in modern cultural and political life. "Nation" is so central, and protean, a category of modern political and cultural thought, discourse, and practice that it is hard indeed to imagine a world without nationalism. But precisely because nationalism is so protean and polymorphous, it makes little sense to ask how strong nationalism is, or whether it is receding or advancing.
>
> – Rogers Brubaker, *Nationalism Reframed: Nationhood and the National Question in the New Europe*

A number of important books by the Canadian School conclude with chapters on unity or some equivalent idea. For example, the last chapter of Taylor's *The Malaise of Modernity* is titled "Against Fragmentation," and the concluding chapters of Will Kymlicka's *Finding Our Way* and *Multicultural Citizenship* are titled, respectively, "The Bonds of Social Unity" and "The Ties That Bind."[1] This placement is interesting, since these conclusions are hardly afterthoughts. Instead, unity considerations drive Taylor and Kymlicka's theorizing throughout. In engaging with their work, this book reverses their emphasis (i.e., the bind that ties) and places their unity concerns up front.

For James Tully, who departs from Taylor, Kymlicka, and others in the Canadian School in interesting ways, "unity is a fantasy," and I am inclined to agree.[2] Still, maybe there is unity in the fantasy, insofar as Canadians fantasize together.

Are We There Yet?
The late twentieth and early twenty-first centuries have been marked by many

extraordinary developments. Meech Lake now seems like a distant memory, and events such as Charlottetown – and even the 1995 Quebec referendum – are fading in light of the "New Canada" of Nunavut, the secession reference case, the Clarity Act, the death of Trudeau, and the aftermath of 9/11. After these developments, is the Canadian unity question now history? One of the most intriguing characteristics of this unity question is the manner in which it answers itself in the process of being asked.

Canadians desire a national home space, yet it is never quite actualized, never quite reached, even as it often seems in sight. One of the reasons that the search for a national home space has taken constitutional forms is that it reflects a coming together, an agreement: the place where the "We" is beyond question. The national home space is out of reach, however, because it is beyond political contestation, beyond politics.

Much of the Canadian scholarship on the national question focuses on the difficulties Canadians have had in their pursuit of unity. Sometimes, the emphasis is on the missed signs or the wrong turns, as if to say, this is where it all went wrong – if only Canadians had done this or that instead. At other times, the emphasis is more celebratory: Canadians have come a long way, even if there have been many bumps and potholes throughout the journey. Either way, there is a direction and a destination. It is just a matter of getting there.

Perhaps a better map would help? In this book, I have attempted to demonstrate that Canadian unity is not achieved through efforts to (re)configure the categories, the people(s), that compose the Canadian political community. Each configuration invariably clashes with others, be it pan-Canadian citizenship, equal citizens, equal provinces, asymmetrical federalism, deep diversity, three nations, or another. Nor is unity achieved through attempts to reduce or clarify the overlap between the various nation categories so that they no longer conflict. Such attempts reproduce the problem, which cannot be solved by shuffling the deck of unities and categories. The greater the efforts to find a resolution to the national question, the more fragmented Canadians become. The search for a unifying cement to bind Canadians together generates an unseemly melée of identitarian politics, a festering mix of competing nationalisms.

Home on the Road: Keep Going, We're Here

But perhaps having a map is not really necessary, as long as Canadians continue in their pursuit of one. The journey is successful as long as it continues. There is a need for some ground rules, however, and some understanding of who is along for the ride. And so the journey continues, unable to move beyond these preliminaries. The Canadian conversation is premised on agreement on the identities of the participants, even as it is driven by contestation over these identities. Is it enough that Canadians are dis/united in their concern with unity, in the value that they place on reaching an agreement over the constitution of their political community? It depends, of course, on whom you ask.

This terrain can be approached in other ways. Instead of an alternative route home, there are alternatives to the dreams of home. Such alternatives do not look to a place beyond politics, where differences may settle, but instead to politics.

But what does "politics" actually look like and how might Canadians get there, especially if they cannot first agree on who they are or where there is (or, indeed, where they have come from)? With questions such as these, they quickly return to familiar ground, as if to say, keep going, we're here! So is this the answer – home on the road? Again, it depends on whom you ask.

For some, Canadian politics, especially constitutional politics, is best understood as a "living tree." Such politics thrives on the pursuit of common roots; once these roots are found, Canadians may then, despite their differences, at least grasp hold of the same trunk. However, the tree that many Canadians grasp is anchored by the *common pursuit* of roots, not by common roots themselves, since there are none.

As an alternative to this "arboreal" politics, Canadians may question the question and partake in "rhizomatic" politics instead, with its combination of underground nodes and shoots. Rhizomes are disorienting, to be sure, because there is no place to begin – or end. Without a map, a clear route, common guidelines, or destination, Canadians would no doubt find themselves lost at times. But who knows what they might discover as they engage in politics with one another in the spaces in-between. To help them along, I turn to Deleuze and Guattari, with a passage that continues in the epigraph of Chapter 1:

> A rhizome has no beginning or end; it is always in the middle, between things, interbeing, intermezzo. The tree is filiation, but the rhizome is alliance, uniquely alliance. The tree imposes the verb "to be," but the fabric of the rhizome is the conjunction, "and ... and ... and ..." The middle is by no means an average; on the contrary, it is where things pick up speed. *Between* things ...

Notes

Chapter 1: The Bind That Ties

1 Although this term is drawn from Jeremy Webber, he would disagree with my usage, as I discuss in Chapter 2. Webber, *Reimagining Canada: Language, Culture, Community, and the Canadian Constitution* (Montreal and Kingston: McGill-Queen's University Press, 1994).
2 Tod Gitlin, *The Twilight of Common Dreams: Why America Is Wracked by Culture Wars* (New York: Henry Holt and Company, 1995).
3 Allan Smith, "Metaphor and Nationality in North America," *Canadian Historical Review* 51, 3 (September 1970): 272; Kogila Moodley, "Canadian Multiculturalism As Ideology," *Ethnic and Racial Studies* 6, 3 (1983): 320-31.
4 See "Canada's New Spirit," *Economist*, 27 September 2003, 15; Pico Iyer, "Imagining Canada: An Outsider's Hope for a Global Future" (Inaugural Hart House Lecture, Toronto, 5 April 2001).
5 When I speak of multiculturalism, I am referring to a broad set of strategies designed to govern diversity rather than to the multiculturalism policy, which is only one such strategy. My use of the word *multicultural* is thus not limited to questions of race, ethnicity, religion, or culture but also extends to struggles involving Quebec, Aboriginal peoples, women, and other marginalized groups.
6 Erin Anderssen and Michael Valpy, *The New Canada: A Globe and Mail Report on the Next Generation* (Toronto: McClelland and Stewart, 2004).
7 Ian Angus, *A Border Within: National Identity, Cultural Plurality, and Wilderness* (Montreal and Kingston: McGill-Queen's University Press, 1997); Joel Bakan, *Just Words: Constitutional Rights, Social Wrongs* (Toronto: University of Toronto Press, 1997); Himani Bannerji, *The Dark Side of the Nation: Essays on Multiculturalism, Nationalism and Gender* (Toronto: Canadian Scholars' Press, 2000); Richard J.F. Day, *Multiculturalism and the History of Canadian Diversity* (Toronto: University of Toronto Press, 2000); Yasmeen Abu-Laban and Christina Gabriel, *Selling Diversity: Immigration, Multiculturalism, Employment Equity, and Globalization* (Peterborough, ON: Broadview Press, 2002); Eva Mackey, *The House of Difference: Cultural Politics and National Identity in Canada* (London: Routledge, 1999); Sherene H. Razack, *Looking White People in the Eye* (Toronto: University of Toronto Press, 1998).
8 For the Aboriginal conversation, see Patricia Monture-Angus, *Journeying Forward: Dreaming First Nations' Independence* (Halifax: Fernwood, 1999); Taiaiake Alfred,

Peace, Power, Righteousness: An Indigenous Manifesto (Toronto: Oxford University Press, 1999); Claude Denis, *We Are Not You: First Nations and Canadian Modernity* (Peterborough, ON: Broadview, 1997); Daniel Salée, "Identities in Conflict: The Aboriginal Question and the Politics of Recognition in Quebec," *Ethnic and Racial Studies* 18, 2 (1995): 277-314. For the gay and lesbian conversation, see Becki Ross, "A Lesbian Politics of Erotic Decolonization," in *Painting the Maple: Essays on Race, Gender, and the Construction of Canada*, ed. Veronica Strong-Boag et al. (Vancouver: UBC Press, 1998); and the collection of essays edited by Terry Goldie, *In a Queer Country: Gay and Lesbian Studies in the Canadian Context* (Vancouver: Arsenal Pulp Press, 2001). For the Québécois conversation, see Jocelyn Maclure, *Quebec Identity: The Challenge of Pluralism*, trans. Peter Feldstein (Montreal and Kingston: McGill-Queen's University Press, 2003); and Michel Venne, ed., *Vive Quebec! New Thinking and New Approaches to the Quebec Nation*, trans. Robert Chodos and Louisa Blair (Toronto: James Lorimer and Company, 2001). For the feminist conversation, see Jo-Anne Lee and Linda Cardinal, "Hegemonic Nationalism and the Politics of Feminism in Canada," in *Painting the Maple*, ed. Strong-Boag et al., 215-41.

9   Richard Day discusses the "problem of the problem of diversity" in *Multiculturalism and the History of Canadian Diversity*. Ronald Beiner and Wayne Norman discuss the emergence of the Canadian School in the introduction to their edited volume, *Canadian Political Philosophy: Contemporary Reflections* (Toronto: Oxford University Press, 2001); for a similar list of Canadian School members, see Ignatieff, *Rights Revolution*, 11. Important works include Charles Taylor, *Reconciling the Solitudes: Essays on Canadian Federalism and Nationalism*, ed. Guy Laforest (Montreal and Kingston: McGill-Queen's University Press, 1993); Charles Taylor, "The Politics of Recognition," in *Multiculturalism: Examining the Politics of Recognition*, ed. Amy Gutmann, 25-73 (Princeton: Princeton University Press, 1994); Will Kymlicka, *Finding Our Way: Rethinking Ethnocultural Relations in Canada* (Toronto: Oxford University Press, 1998); Joseph Carens, *Culture, Citizenship, and Community: A Contextual Exploration of Justice As Evenhandedness* (Oxford: Oxford University Press, 2000); Simone Chambers, "New Constitutionalism: Democracy, Habermas, and Canadian Exceptionalism," in Beiner and Norman, *Canadian Political Philosophy*; Michael Ignatieff, *The Rights Revolution* (Toronto: Anansi, 2000); James Tully, *Strange Multiplicity: Constitutionalism in an Age of Diversity* (Cambridge: Cambridge University Press, 1995); and Webber, *Reimagining Canada*.

10 Ruth Abbey, *Charles Taylor* (Princeton: Princeton University Press, 2000); Nicholas H. Smith, *Charles Taylor: Meaning, Morals, and Modernity* (Malden, MA: Polity Press, 2002); and James Tully, ed., *Philosophy in an Age of Pluralism: The Philosophy of Charles Taylor in Question* (Cambridge: Cambridge University Press, 1994).

11 Brian Barry, *Culture and Equality: An Egalitarian Critique of Multiculturalism* (Cambridge, MA: Harvard University Press, 1999); Seyla Benhabib, *The Claims of Culture: Equality and Diversity in the Global Era* (Princeton, NJ: Princeton University Press, 2002); Amy Gutmann, *Identity in Democracy* (Princeton, NJ: Princeton University Press, 2004); Bhiku C. Parekh, *Rethinking Multiculturalism: Cultural Diversity and Political Theory* (Cambridge, MA: Harvard University Press, 2000).

12 See *Federalism and the French Canadians* (Toronto: Macmillan, 1968); *Conversations with Canadians* (Toronto: University of Toronto Press, 1972). Of the numerous "Trudeauite" scholars, Ramsay Cook is especially sophisticated: *Canada,*

Québec, and the Uses of Nationalism, 2nd ed. (Toronto: McClelland and Stewart, 1995).

13 On the "equality" side, beyond the Trudeauites, see Janet Ajzenstat, "Liberalism and Assimilation: Lord Durham Reconsidered," in *Political Thought in Canada,* ed. Stephen Brooks, 239-57 (Toronto: Irwin Publishing, 1984); David J. Bercuson and Barry Cooper, *Deconfederation: Canada without Quebec* (Toronto: Key Porter Books, 1991); Reginald W. Bibby, *Mosaic Madness: The Poverty and Potential of Life in Canada* (Toronto: Stoddart, 1990); Tom Flanagan, *First Nations? Second Thoughts* (Montreal and Kingston: McGill-Queen's University Press, 2000); and Richard Gwyn, *Nationalism without Walls: The Unbearable Lightness of Being Canadian* (Toronto: McClelland and Stewart, 1995). On the "difference" side, beyond the Canadian School, see Alan C. Cairns, *Citizens Plus: Aboriginal Peoples and the Canadian State* (Vancouver: UBC Press, 2000); Kenneth McRoberts, *Misconceiving Canada: The Struggle for National Unity* (Toronto: Oxford University Press, 1997); Beverley McLachlin, "The Civilization of Difference" (Fourth Annual Lafontaine-Baldwin Lecture, Halifax, March 2003) <www.operation-dialogue.com/lafontaine-baldwin> (4 November 2004); Philip Resnick, *Thinking English Canada* (Toronto: Stoddart, 1994); and Peter Russell, *Constitutional Odyssey: Can Canadians Become a Sovereign People?* (Toronto: University of Toronto Press, 2004).

14 At various points, I utilize television news transcripts taken during the Charlottetown referendum campaign (3 September-25 October 1992). Included in these transcripts are all the reports (news stories, editorial essays, documentaries, interviews, debates, and "town hall meetings") that make any reference to the referendum. This amounts to fifty-two consecutive evenings of newscasts including 172 stories from the CBC news program *The National,* 39 from CBC's *The Journal,* 36 from CBC's *Sunday Report,* and 181 from the *CTV News.* Transcripts were provided by the National Media Archives.

15 Kymlicka, *Finding Our Way;* Resnick, *Thinking English Canada;* Reg Whitaker, "With or without Quebec?" in *"English Canada" Speaks Out,* ed. J.L. Granatstein and Kenneth McNaught (Toronto: Doubleday Canada, 1991); Angus, *Border Within.*

16 H.B. Hawthorn and M.A. Tremblay, *A Survey of the Contemporary Indians of Canada: A Report on Economic, Political, Educational Needs and Policies* (Ottawa: Queen's Printers, 1966); Department of Indian Affairs and Northern Development, *Statement of the Government of Canada on Indian Policy* (Ottawa, 1969).

17 For example, Harold Cardinal, *The Unjust Society: The Tragedy of Canada's Indians* (Edmonton: Hurtig Publishing, 1969).

18 Martha Minow, *Making All the Difference: Inclusion, Exclusion, and American Law* (Ithaca, NY: Cornell University Press, 1990).

19 Joseph Carens makes this distinction in "Dimensions of Citizenship and National Identity in Canada," *Philosophical Forum* 28, 1-2 (1996-7): 111-24.

20 Will Kymlicka makes this distinction in "Three Forms of Group-Differentiated Citizenship in Canada," in *Democracy and Difference: Contesting the Boundaries of the Political,* ed. Seyla Benhabib (Princeton: Princeton University Press, 1996).

Chapter 2: Confounding Debates

1 Peter H. Russell, *Constitutional Odyssey: Can Canadians Become a Sovereign People?* (Toronto: University of Toronto Press, 2004).

2 Simone Chambers, "New Constitutionalism: Democracy, Habermas, and Canadian Exceptionalism," in *Canadian Political Philosophy: Contemporary Reflections,*

ed. Ronald Beiner and Wayne Norman (Toronto: Oxford University Press, 2001); Will Kymlicka, *Finding Our Way: Rethinking Ethnocultural Relations in Canada* (Toronto: Oxford University Press, 1998), ch. 13; Charles Taylor, *Reconciling the Solitudes: Essays on Canadian Federalism and Nationalism*, ed. Guy Laforest (Montreal and Kingston: McGill-Queen's University Press, 1993); James Tully, "Diversity's Gambit Declined," in *Constitutional Predicament: Canada after the Referendum of 1992*, ed. Curtis Cook (Montreal and Kingston: McGill-Queen's University Press, 1994); James Tully, *Strange Multiplicity: Constitutionalism in an Age of Diversity* (Cambridge: Cambridge University Press, 1995); Jeremy Webber, *Reimagining Canada: Language, Culture, Community, and the Canadian Constitution* (Montreal and Kingston: McGill-Queen's University Press, 1994). For further discussion, see Charles Blattberg, *Shall We Dance? A Patriotic Politics for Canada* (Montreal and Kingston: McGill-Queen's University Press, 2003).
3 Webber, *Reimagining Canada*, 185-6.
4 Chambers, "New Constitutionalism," 69-70.
5 What follows should be distinguished from the rules governing Habermasian discourse theory.
6 At minimum, this majoritarianism is English Canadian, although it is often far broader. I discuss English Canadian nationalism in Chapter 5.
7 This is far from straightforward. The presence of René Lévesque during the negotiations on the patriation of the Constitution and the question of whether he was "on the same page" as the other first ministers is central to the continuing disagreement over the so-called night of the long knives, and whether Quebec's decision not to sign the Constitution Act, 1982 was a result of this betrayal or merely a logical consequence of Lévesque's separatist politics.
8 For a recent illustration of this narrative of liberal progress, see Supreme Court Chief Justice Beverley McLachlin's lecture, "The Civilization of Difference" (Fourth Annual Lafontaine-Baldwin Lecture, Halifax, 7 March 2003), <www.operation-dialogue.com/lafontaine-baldwin> (4 November 2004). In *Multiculturalism and the History of Canadian Diversity*, Richard Day provides an excellent examination of the history of Canadian state discourses concerning diversity.
9 G.M. Craig, ed., *An Abridgement of the Report on the Affairs of British North America by Lord Durham* (Ottawa: Carleton University Press, 1982); Department of Indian Affairs and Northern Development, *Statement of the Government of Canada on Indian Policy* (Ottawa, 1969).
10 "Premiers' Framework for Discussion on Canadian Unity" [Calgary Declaration], 14 September 1997.
11 Bhiku C. Parekh, *Rethinking Multiculturalism: Cultural Diversity and Political Theory* (Cambridge, MA: Harvard University Press, 2000), 231-2.
12 Appearance is key here: I am not suggesting that the Canadian political identity is actually neutral or empty but only that it is put forward as if it were.
13 As Kogila Moodley argues, "In a country with a vague identity, in a society rich in geography and short of history, multiculturalism is propagated as the lowest common denominator on which all segments may agree." "Canadian Multiculturalism As Ideology," *Ethnic and Racial Studies* 6, 3 (1983): 329. In addition, see Allan Smith, "Metaphor and Nationality," *Canadian Historical Review* 51, 3 (1970): 272.
14 Arthur M. Schlesinger Jr., *The Disuniting of America: Reflections on a Multicultural Society*, rev. ed. (New York: W.W. Norton and Company, 1998), 17.

15 Michael Ignatieff discusses this attention in *The Rights Revolution* (Toronto: Anansi, 2000), ch. 1.
16 To provide just one of many possible examples, J.R. Miller argues that the early answer to the question of what would hold Canada together was John A. Macdonald's centralism, and especially "the gargantuan task of binding the newly acquired and sparsely populated West to the rest of the country with a transcontinental railway." "Unity/Diversity: The Canadian Experience: From Confederation to the First World War," in *Readings in Canadian History: Post-Confederation*, ed. R. Douglas Francis and Donald B. Smith, 4th ed. (Toronto: Harcourt Brace and Company Canada, 1994).
17 Jürgen Habermas, "The European Nation-State: On the Past and Future of Sovereignty and Citizenship," in *The Inclusion of the Other: Studies in Political Theory* (Cambridge, MA: MIT Press, 1998), 118.
18 Chambers, "New Constitutionalism," 69.
19 Lorraine Code, *What Can She Know?* (Ithaca, NY: Cornell University Press, 1991), 29.
20 For discussions of the role of the equality/difference dichotomy in feminist theorizing, see Joan W. Scott, "Deconstructing Equality-Versus-Difference: Or the Uses of Poststructuralist Theory for Feminism," in *Conflicts in Feminism*, ed. Marianne Hirsch and Evelyn Fox Keller (New York: Routledge, 1990); and Gisela Bock and Susan James, eds., *Beyond Equality and Difference: Citizenship, Feminist Politics and Female Subjectivity* (London: Routledge, 1992), especially the essay by Carole Pateman, "Equality, Difference, Subordination: The Politics of Motherhood and Women's Citizenship."
21 Nancy Fraser, *Justice Interruptus: Critical Reflections on the "Postsocialist" Condition* (New York: Routledge, 1997), 186-7.
22 See, in particular, Iris Marion Young, "Unruly Categories: A Critique of Nancy Fraser's Dual Systems Theory," *New Left Review* 222 (1997): 147-60; the response from Fraser, "A Rejoinder to Iris Young," *New Left Review* 223 (1997): 126-9; Judith Butler, "Merely Cultural," *New Left Review* 227 (1998): 33-44; and another response from Fraser, "Heterosexism, Misrecognition and Capitalism: A Response to Judith Butler," *New Left Review* 228 (1998): 140-9. For further discussion of this debate, see Leah F. Vosko, "The Pasts (and Futures) of Feminist Political Economy in Canada: Reviving the Debate," in *Studies in Political Economy: Developments in Feminism*, ed. Caroline Andrew et al. (Toronto: Women's Press, 2003).
23 Joan W. Scott, "The Sears Case," in *Gender and the Politics of History* (New York: Columbia University Press, 1988), 172. See also Scott, "Deconstructing Equality-Versus-Difference"; and Wendy Brown, *States of Injury: Power and Freedom in Late Modernity* (Princeton: Princeton University Press, 1995), 153-4, 165.
24 Scott, "Sears Case," 168.
25 Scott, "Deconstructing Equality-Versus-Difference," 142.
26 Will Kymlicka, *Multicultural Citizenship: A Liberal Theory of Minority Rights* (Oxford: Oxford University Press, 1995); James Tully, *Strange Multiplicity;* and Charles Taylor, "Shared and Divergent Values," in *Reconciling the Solitudes*.
27 According to Code, "The dissolution of a dichotomy does not render its terms meaningless. Rather, it denies both terms the absolute force that the oppositional structure of the dichotomy confers." *What Can She Know?* 30.
28 Scott, "Deconstructing Equality-Versus-Difference," 142.

29 Bonnie Honig, "Difference, Dilemmas and the Politics of Home," in *Democracy and Difference: Contesting the Boundaries of the Political*, ed. Seyla Benhabib (Princeton: Princeton University Press, 1996), 258.
30 Webber, *Reimagining Canada*, 26.
31 Kenneth McRoberts, *Misconceiving Canada: The Struggle for National Unity* (Toronto: Oxford University Press, 1997).
32 Tully, "Diversity's Gambit Declined," 161.
33 Ibid., 165.
34 Ibid., 161-2.
35 For discussions of what such a creative politics might look like, see Gad Horowitz, "Toward the Democratic Class Struggle," in *Agenda 1970: Proposals for a Creative Politics*, ed. Trevor Lloyd and Jack McLeod (Toronto: University of Toronto Press, 1968); Homi K. Bhabha, *The Location of Culture* (London: Routledge, 1994); and Judith Butler, Ernesto Laclau, and Slavoj Žižek, *Contingency, Hegemony, Universality: Contemporary Dialogues on the Left* (London: Verso, 2000).

Chapter 3: Just Nationalism?

1 Michael Ignatieff, *The Rights Revolution* (Toronto: Anansi, 2000); for an earlier treatment by Ignatieff, see *Blood and Belonging: Journeys into the New Nationalism* (Toronto: Penguin Books, 1993), 168-9.
2 Peter H. Russell, "The Political Purposes of the Canadian Charter of Rights and Freedoms," *Canadian Bar Review* 61 (1983): 30; Rainer Knopff and F.L. Morton, *Charter Politics* (Toronto: Nelson Canada, 1992), ch. 13; Guy Laforest, *Trudeau and the End of a Canadian Dream*, trans. Paul Leduc Browne and Michelle Weinroth (Montreal and Kingston: McGill-Queen's University Press, 1995).
3 Ignatieff, *Rights Revolution*, 77-8.
4 Ramsay Cook, *Canada and the French-Canadian Question* (Toronto: Macmillan, 1966), 146.
5 Avigail Eisenberg has critiqued those who interpret Aboriginal/non-Aboriginal relations in this way. She argues that "the common characterization that Canada's governing and representative institutions are viewed as illegitimate among Aboriginal peoples because Aboriginal peoples subscribe to collectivism while Canadian political institutions reflect individualism is mistaken, and, further, it is insidious." "Domination and Political Representation in Canada," in *Painting the Maple: Essays on Race, Gender, and the Construction of Canada*, ed. Veronica Strong-Boag et al. (Vancouver: UBC Press, 1998), 49. In contrast, Darlene M. Johnston operates within the parameters of the liberal/communitarian divide. "Native Rights As Collective Rights: A Question of Group Self-Preservation," in *The Rights of Minority Cultures*, ed. Will Kymlicka (Oxford: Oxford University Press, 1995). For further discussion, see Mary Ellen Turpel, "The Charlottetown Discord and Aboriginal Peoples' Struggles for Fundamental Political Change," in *The Charlottetown Accord, the Referendum, and the Future of Canada*, ed. Kenneth McRoberts and Patrick Monahan (Toronto: University of Toronto Press, 1993), 135-8.
6 This is the framing presented in the popular *Crosscurrents* undergraduate textbook. The "Yes" answer is by Pierre Trudeau, "Values in a Just Society," and the "No" answer by Paul Marshall, "The Importance of Group Rights." Mark Charlton and Paul Barker, eds., *Crosscurrents: Contemporary Political Issues*, 4th ed. (Toronto: Nelson, 2002), ch. 2.

7 Charles Taylor, "Shared and Divergent Values," in *Reconciling the Solitudes: Essays on Canadian Federalism and Nationalism*, ed. Guy Laforest (Montreal and Kingston: McGill-Queen's University Press, 1993); and "The Politics of Recognition," in *Multiculturalism: Examining the Politics of Recognition*, ed. Amy Gutmann (Princeton: Princeton University Press, 1994). There are some overlapping passages between the two essays. Taylor also covers some of the same ground in his 1991 Massey Lectures, published as *The Malaise of Modernity* (Concord, ON: Anansi, 1991), and in his Macdonald Commission essay, "Alternative Futures: Legitimacy, Identity, and Alienation in Late Twentieth Century Canada," in *Constitutionalism, Citizenship and Society in Canada*, ed. Alan Cairns and Cynthia Williams, 183-230 (Toronto: University of Toronto Press, 1985). Taylor's interpretation of the Canadian impasse has been discussed by, among many others, Janet Ajzenstat, "Decline of Procedural Liberalism: The Slippery Slope to Secession," in *Is Quebec Nationalism Just? Perspectives from Anglophone Canada*, ed. Joseph H. Carens, 120-5 (Montreal and Kingston: McGill-Queen's University Press, 1995); Ramsay Cook, "Nation, Identity, Rights: Reflections on W.L. Morton's *The Canadian Identity*," in *Canada, Québec and the Uses of Nationalism*, 2nd ed. (Toronto: McClelland and Stewart, 1995); Ian Angus, *A Border Within: National Identity, Cultural Plurality, and Wilderness* (Montreal and Kingston: McGill-Queen's University Press, 1997), ch. 6; and Guy Laforest, "Philosophy and Political Judgment in a Multinational Federation," in *Philosophy in an Age of Pluralism: The Philosophy of Charles Taylor in Question*, ed. James Tully (Cambridge: Cambridge University Press, 1994).

8 Taylor speaks of "substantive liberalism" instead of "communitarianism," reframing the gulf that divides Quebec from the rest of Canada within liberal terms, as I will discuss. Taylor also prefers the term "Canada outside Quebec" (or COQ) to "English Canada." I use the latter term because I believe that doing otherwise obscures the political relations at issue, and because COQ includes Aboriginal and other communities that often make the kind of claims put forward by Quebec.

9 Gad Horowitz, "Conservatism, Liberalism, and Socialism in Canada: An Interpretation," *Canadian Journal of Economic and Political Science* 32, 2 (May 1966): 143-71. Horowitz responds to some of his critics in "Notes on Conservatism, Liberalism and Socialism in Canada," *Canadian Journal of Political Science* 11, 2 (1978): 383-99.

10 The list of secondary literature on the Hartz/Horowitz thesis is a long one. See, in particular, Donald Forbes, "Hartz/Horowitz at Twenty: Nationalism, Toryism and Socialism in Canada and the United States," *Canadian Journal of Political Science* 20, 2 (1987): 287-315; and Nelson Wiseman, "A Note on 'Hartz-Horowitz at Twenty': The Case of French Canada," *Canadian Journal of Political Science* 21 (December 1988): 795-806.

11 See, in particular, the first chapter by Janet Ajzenstat and Peter J. Smith in their edited collection, "Liberal-Republicanism: The Revisionist Picture of Canada's Founding," *Canada's Origins: Liberal, Tory, or Republican?* (Ottawa: Carleton University Press, 1995), 1-18.

12 Ibid., 11. I would argue that the Canadian textbooks are more likely to emphasize individual/collectivist-type interpretations. Ironically, the same undergraduate textbook noted above (for its section on individual and collective rights) contains another section asking, "Are Canadians tory-touched liberals?" with the "Yes" response by Nelson Wiseman and the "No" response drawn from Ajzenstat and Smith. Charlton and Barker, *Crosscurrents*, ch. 3.

13 Janet Ajzenstat herself is another exception. See *The Political Thought of Lord Durham* (Montreal and Kingston: McGill-Queen's University Press, 1988) and the chapters in Part 4 of Ajzenstat and Smith, *Canada's Origins*.
14 Taylor, "Politics of Recognition," 43.
15 Ibid., 39.
16 Ibid., 48-9.
17 Ibid., 50-1.
18 Taylor, "Shared and Divergent Values," 157-70.
19 Ibid., 174-7.
20 Ibid., 165.
21 In the Meech Lake Accord, the full wording of the distinct society clause is as follows: "The Constitution of Canada shall be interpreted in a manner consistent with (a) the recognition that the existence of French-speaking Canadians, centred in Quebec but also present elsewhere in Canada, and English-speaking Canadians, concentrated outside Quebec but also present in the province, constitutes a fundamental characteristic of Canada; and (b) the recognition that Quebec constitutes within Canada a distinct society." Constitution Amendment, 1987 [Meech Lake Accord] (Ottawa: Ministry of Supply and Services, 3 June 1987).
22 Samuel LaSelva, *The Moral Foundations of Canadian Federalism: Paradoxes, Achievements, and Tragedies of Nationhood* (Montreal and Kingston: McGill-Queen's University Press, 1996), 125.
23 Taylor, "Shared and Divergent Values," 172.
24 Ibid., 178.
25 These include the ability to deny mobility rights in certain instances (s. 6.4); Aboriginal and treaty rights (s. 25 and s. 35); multicultural rights (s. 27); and the override or "notwithstanding clause" (s. 33). For discussion, see Michael Hartney, "Some Confusions Concerning Collective Rights," in *The Rights of Minority Cultures*, ed. Will Kymlicka (Oxford: Oxford University Press, 1995), 220. See also Cook, "Nation, Identity, Rights," 234. One could also argue that the Charter's preamble referring to the "supremacy of God" violates procedural liberal principles.
26 On the positive side, see Beverley McLachlin, "The Civilization of Difference" (Fourth Annual Lafontaine-Baldwin Lecture, Halifax, March 2003), <www.operation-dialogue.com/lafontaine-baldwin> (4 November 2004); on the negative side, see F.L. Morton and Rainer Knopff, *The Charter Revolution and the Court Party* (Toronto: Broadview, 2000).
27 Section 15(1) of the Charter says, "Every individual is equal before and under the law," and section 15(2) says, "Subsection (1) does not preclude any law, program, or activity that has as its object the amelioration of conditions of disadvantaged individuals or groups including those that are disadvantaged because of race, national or ethnic origin, colour, religion, sex, age or mental or physical ability." Canadian Charter of Rights and Freedoms, Part I of the Constitution Act, 1982, being Schedule B to the Canada Act 1982 (U.K.), 1982, c. 11.
28 Ignatieff, *Rights Revolution*, 7-8; and Simone Chambers, "New Constitutionalism: Democracy, Habermas, and Canadian Exceptionalism," in *Canadian Political Philosophy: Contemporary Reflections*, ed. Ronald Beiner and Wayne Norman (Toronto: Oxford University Press, 2001). Thomas Berger, although not referring to Taylor here, sums up the point rather forcefully: "The idiotic idea that the Charter enshrines English Canada's individualistic notions of our polity, but does not recognize collectivities, and that Quebec rejects the Charter on that ground,

could only occur to anyone who has never read the Charter. It protects both." "Quebec's Rendezvous with Independence," in *"English Canada" Speaks Out*, ed. J.L. Granatstein and Kenneth McNaught (Toronto: Doubleday Canada, 1991), 318.
29 Taylor, "Shared and Divergent Values," 172.
30 In 1989 the Equality Party of Quebec was formed in order to mobilize against Bill 178. According to the party's website, "Equality is a *civil rights* party dedicated to protecting all Quebecers of *all* ethnic and linguistic groups." Notably, the party rejected the DSC because it would encourage "the erosion of civil rights in Quebec," *as well as* because "the equality of the provinces would be adversely affected." Equality Party website, <www.equality.qc.ca> (2 March 2000). See also Mordecai Richler, *Oh Canada! Oh Quebec! Requiem for a Divided Country* (Toronto: Penguin, 1992).
31 Kenneth McRoberts, *Misconceiving Canada: The Struggle for National Unity* (Toronto: Oxford University Press, 1997), 202-3.
32 To complicate matters further, some of the most vocal rights-based critics of the DSC in English Canada were feminist groups, such as the National Action Committee on the Status of Women (NAC), concerned that the clause would undermine women's equality rights; this was especially evident during the Charlottetown Round. Yet NAC is far from proceduralist in orientation, nor does it object to giving additional powers to Quebec, with certain qualifications, so that it can preserve and develop its culture. National Action Committee on the Status of Women, "NAC's Response to the Report of the Special Joint Committee on 'A Renewed Canada' (Beaudoin-Dobbie)," Toronto, May 1992; and "NAC says 'NO': The Charlottetown Agreement Threatens Equality Rights," Toronto, 1992. Robert Vipond makes a similar point in "From Provincial Autonomy to Provincial Equality (Or, Clyde Wells and the Distinct Society)," in *Is Quebec Nationalism Just? Perspectives from Anglophone Canada*, ed. Joseph Carens (Montreal and Kingston: McGill-Queen's University Press, 1995), 111.
33 Ajzenstat, "Decline of Procedural Liberalism," 129.
34 As an indication of this, consider the range of critiques of the Charter presented by Richard Sigurdson, "Left- and Right-Wing Charterphobia in Canada: A Critique of the Critics," *International Journal of Canadian Studies* 7-8 (1993): 95-115.
35 Alan Cairns has made this argument in a number of essays, for example, "Constitutional Minoritarianism in Canada," in *Reconfigurations: Canadian Citizenship and Constitutional Change*, ed. Douglas E. Williams, 119-41 (Toronto: McClelland and Stewart, 1995); also see F.L. Morton and Rainer Knopff, *The Charter Revolution and the Court Party* (Peterborough, ON: Broadview Press, 2000).
36 Michael Mandel, *The Charter of Rights and the Legalization of Politics in Canada*, rev. ed. (Toronto: Thompson Educational Publishing, 1994). Sherene Razack is somewhat more optimistic about the radical possibilities of Charter-based strategies, in *Canadian Feminism and the Law: The Women's Legal Education and Action Fund and the Pursuit of Equality* (Toronto: Second Story Press, 1991).
37 Joseph Carens, "Immigration, Political Community, and the Transformation of Identity: Quebec's Immigration Policies in Critical Perspective," in Carens, *Is Quebec Nationalism Just?* 72-4.
38 Laforest, "Philosophy and Political Judgment," 204.

39 Louis Balthazar, "Identity and Nationalism in Quebec," in *Clash of Identities: Essays on Media, Manipulation, and Politics of the Self*, ed. James Littleton (Toronto: Prentice Hall, 1996), 102.
40 Cook, "Nation, Identity, Rights," 234.
41 Taylor, "Shared and Divergent Values," 174, emphasis added.
42 John Rawls, *A Theory of Justice* (Cambridge, MA: Belknap Press of Harvard University Press, 1971), 24; see also Ronald Dworkin, *Taking Rights Seriously* (Cambridge, MA: Harvard University Press, 1977), 171-7.
43 Dworkin, *Taking Rights Seriously*, 227.
44 In Taylor's more philosophical treatment of the procedural/substantive distinction, he views procedural liberalism as inevitably resting on a substantive vision of the good because it is otherwise incoherent: "What makes it mandatory to follow the privileged procedures? The answer has to lie in some understanding of human life and reason, in some positive doctrine of man, and hence the good. It is greatly to the credit of Kant that he recognizes this and spells out his view of man, or rather rational agency, and the dignity that attaches to it, that is, what makes it of infinitely higher worth than anything else in the universe." "The Motivation behind a Procedural Ethics," in *Kant and Political Philosophy: The Contemporary Legacy*, ed. Ronald Beiner and William James Booth (New Haven: Yale University Press, 1993), 349.
45 Paul M. Sniderman et al. make a similar point, suggesting that "group rights are about groups, not rights, and this applies both to those who favor them and those who reject them. Their natural effect, therefore, is to sharpen cleavages between groups, whether one has in mind the group that loses under them or the group that benefits from them." *The Clash of Rights: Liberty, Equality, and Legitimacy in Pluralist Democracy* (New Haven: Yale University Press, 1996), 250.
46 Ignatieff, *Rights Revolution*; McLachlin, "Civilization of Difference."

Chapter 4: Decoding Deep Diversity
1 A few of the many discussions include Daiva Stasiulis, "'Deep Diversity': Race and Ethnicity in Canadian Politics," in *Canadian Politics in the 1990s*, ed. Michael S. Whittington and Glen Williams, 4th ed. (Scarborough, ON: Nelson Canada, 1995), 211-12; Joseph Carens, "Citizenship and the Challenge of Aboriginal Self-Government: Is Deep Diversity Desirable?" ch. 8 of *Culture, Citizenship, and Community: A Contextual Exploration of Justice As Evenhandedness* (Oxford: Oxford University Press, 2000); and Will Kymlicka and Wayne Norman, "Return of the Citizen: A Survey of Recent Work on Citizenship Theory," in *Theorizing Citizenship*, ed. Ronald Beiner (Albany: SUNY Press, 1995), 308-9.
2 For extended discussions of Canadian constitutional politics, see Peter H. Russell, *Constitutional Odyssey: Can Canadians Become a Sovereign People?* (Toronto: University of Toronto Press, 2004); Alan C. Cairns, *Disruptions: Constitutional Struggles, from the Charter to Meech Lake*, ed. Douglas E. Williams (Toronto: McClelland and Stewart, 1991); Patrick J. Monahan, *Meech Lake: The Inside Story* (Toronto: University of Toronto Press, 1991); Michael Behiels, ed., *The Meech Lake Primer: Conflicting Views of the 1987 Constitutional Accord* (Ottawa: University of Ottawa Press, 1989); Kenneth McRoberts and Patrick Monahan, eds., *The Charlottetown Accord, the Referendum, and the Future of Canada* (Toronto: University of Toronto Press, 1993).

3 These five demands were "the explicit recognition of Québec as a distinct society; a guarantee of increased powers in immigration matters; the limitation of federal spending power; recognition of a right to veto; Québec's participation in the appointment of judges to the Supreme Court of Canada." Gil Rémillard, "Quebec's Quest for Survival and Equality via the Meech Lake Accord," in Behiels, *Meech Lake Primer*, 29.
4 The distribution of powers within the federal level is somewhat more complicated, since it represents a zero-sum game where seats in the House of Commons are concerned.
5 David Milne, "Equality or Asymmetry: Why Choose?" in *Options for a New Canada*, ed. Ronald L. Watts and Douglas M. Brown (Toronto: University of Toronto Press, 1991), 297. See also Jeremy Webber, who discusses equal citizenship and the Meech Lake Accord at some length in *Reimagining Canada: Language, Culture, Community, and the Canadian Constitution* (Montreal and Kingston: McGill-Queen's University Press, 1994), 141.
6 There were certainly other reasons for the Accord's unpopularity, such as the negotiating process, a form of executive federalism, and the ratification process, in which no amendments would be entertained. See Cairns, "Citizens (Outsiders) and Governments (Insiders) in Constitution-Making: The Case of Meech Lake," in *Disruptions*. The attempts to dilute the distinct society clause are discussed by Milne, "Equality or Asymmetry," 297-8.
7 Charles Taylor, "Shared and Divergent Values," in *Reconciling the Solitudes: Essays on Canadian Federalism and Nationalism*, ed. Guy Laforest (Montreal and Kingston: McGill-Queen's University Press, 1993), 179.
8 Ibid., 180.
9 Ibid., 183.
10 Canada, Charlottetown Accord, draft legal text (Ottawa: Ministry of Supply and Services, 9 October 1992), s. 2(1)(c).
11 Ibid., s. 2(1)(h).
12 Ibid., s. 2(2).
13 Ibid., s. 126A(5).
14 Pierre Elliott Trudeau, *"A Mess That Deserves a Big NO"* (Toronto: Robert Davies Publishing, 1992), 21.
15 *The Journal*, CBC, 16 October 1992, placement 2. Placements indicate the order of the item in the newscast.
16 Rogers Brubaker, "Myths and Misconceptions in the Study of Nationalism," in *National Self-Determination and Secession*, ed. Margaret Moore (Oxford: Oxford University Press, 1998), 233-65.
17 Richard Simeon and Mary Janigan, eds., *Toolkits and Building Blocks: Constructing a New Canada* (Toronto: C.D. Howe Institute, 1991).
18 Brian Schwartz, "Canada Cannot Be Held Together by Taking It Apart," in *"English Canada" Speaks Out*, ed. J.L. Granatstein and Kenneth McNaught (Toronto: Doubleday Canada, 1991), 342-4.
19 Milne, "Equality or Asymmetry."
20 Taylor, "Shared and Divergent Values," 181, emphasis added.
21 For an interesting discussion of similar manifestations of resentment in the American context, see William Connolly's essay "Fundamentalism in America," in *The Ethos of Pluralization* (Minneapolis: University of Minnesota Press, 1995).

22 "Premiers' Framework for Discussion on Canadian Unity" [Calgary Declaration], 14 September 1997.
23 Graham Fraser and Brian Laghi, "Deal-Making: Harris Steps in to Build Compromise between Two Camps," *Globe and Mail*, 16 September 1997, A1, A4.
24 Bruce Wallace, "The Unity Challenge: The Premiers Try to Reach out to Quebec," *Maclean's*, 29 September 1997, 15.
25 Before the premiers' meeting in Calgary, Reform Party leader Preston Manning wrote to the provincial premiers urging them to develop a common vision in order to "strengthen the unity of the country," insisting that there be "a strong commitment by the federal government to the equality of citizens and provinces in law." At the same time, Manning argued, each province must be given "those tools required to protect and develop the unique features of their economies and societies. This will *ensure that Quebec has the tools needed to protect and develop its unique language, culture, and* civil law tradition." Preston Manning, "Letter to Premiers," 21 July 1997, Reform Party website (accessed November 1997; site now discontinued), emphasis added.
26 Rosemary Speirs, "Chrétien Now Has 2-Track Unity Approach," *Toronto Star*, 16 September 1997, A17.
27 Wallace, "The Unity Challenge." According to *Globe and Mail* columnist Jeffrey Simpson, "Mr. Manning's hand was not on the premiers' pen, but his handwriting is nevertheless all over the document." "The Ghost of 'Distinct Society' Is Still Clanking Its Chains," *Globe and Mail*, 16 September 1997, A16.
28 The single exception to this emphasis that I could find was in a technical paper included on the government of Saskatchewan's "Unity" website, which acknowledged that differential treatment is sometimes necessary: "Equality under the Charter does not necessarily mean sameness of treatment. The law recognizes that in order to guarantee equality for all Canadians it is sometimes necessary to treat individuals in a way that takes into account their unique needs and characteristics. For example, a person who is physically challenged may need special arrangements in the workplace in order to ensure that he or she is treated equally." <www.gov.sk.ca> (9 November 1997).
29 Ibid. The government of Newfoundland presented the matter similarly: "Q. Will there be separate powers for any province? A. No. Principle 6 states clearly that if the Constitution is amended to give a power to one province, that power must be available to all provinces. Principle 5 recognizes that Quebec has a role to protect and develop its unique character, but no special powers are associated with that role." "Backgrounder: The Calgary Declaration – Questions and Answers on Canadian Unity," <www.gov.nl.ca> (9 November 1997).
30 *As It Happens*, CBC Radio, "For the Record," replayed from *Crosstalk*, CBC Radio St. John's, 13 November 1997.
31 *Concise Oxford Dictionary of Current English*, 8th ed.
32 Emphasis added. Government of Saskatchewan website, <www.gov.sk.ca> (9 November 1997).
33 Government of Newfoundland website, <www.gov.nl.ca> (November 1997).
34 For an interesting discussion of the differences between the two terms, see Sandra Martin, "Only in Canada You Say? Our National Taste for a Certain Endless Debate Is Distinctive, Perhaps Even Unique," *Globe and Mail*, 20 September 1997, D6.

35 Preston Manning, "Let the People In: Opposition Leader Calls for Grassroots Voice," guest editorial, *Calgary Herald,* 23 September 1997, A15.
36 Dion quoted in Edison Stewart, "Have Premiers Finally Found Magic Formula?" *Toronto Star,* 20 September 1997, A1.
37 Chrétien quoted in William Walker, "Chrétien Likes Sound of 'Unique': Hails Premiers for Burying 'Distinct Society,'" *Toronto Star,* 16 September 1997, A10.
38 Bouchard quoted in Rhéal Séguin, "Bouchard Reviles Unity Proposal," *Globe and Mail,* 17 September 1997, A4.
39 "Mr Bouchard's Latest Humiliation," *Globe and Mail,* editorial, 18 September 1997, A24.
40 Fontaine quoted in Canadian Press, "Fontaine Attacks Unity Declaration," *Toronto Star,* 4 November 1997, A10.
41 Michel Foucault, "The Eye of Power," interview by Jean-Pierre Barou and Michelle Perrot, in *Power/Knowledge: Selected Interviews and Other Writings 1972-1977,* ed. Colin Gordon (New York: Pantheon, 1980), 152. Iris Marion Young discusses this Foucauldian theme in *Justice and the Politics of Difference* (Princeton: Princeton University Press, 1990), 229.
42 Taylor, "Shared and Divergent Values," 182.

Chapter 5: Nationalisms Disentangled

1 Pierre Trudeau, "New Treason of the Intellectuals," *Federalism and the French Canadians* (Toronto: Macmillan, 1968).
2 Kenneth McRoberts, *Misconceiving Canada: The Struggle for National Unity* (Toronto: Oxford University Press, 1997); Claude Couture, *Paddling with the Current: Pierre Elliott Trudeau, Étienne Parent, Liberalism and Nationalism in Canada,* trans. Vivien Bosley (Edmonton: University of Alberta Press, 1998); Guy Laforest, *Trudeau and the End of a Canadian Dream,* trans. Paul Leduc Browne and Michelle Weinroth (Montreal and Kingston: McGill-Queen's University Press, 1995).
3 Will Kymlicka, *Finding Our Way: Rethinking Ethnocultural Relations in Canada* (Toronto: Oxford University Press, 1998); Philip Resnick, *Thinking English Canada* (Toronto: Stoddart, 1994); Ian Angus, *A Border Within: National Identity, Cultural Plurality, and Wilderness* (Montreal and Kingston: McGill-Queen's University Press, 1997); Reg Whitaker, "With or without Quebec?" in *"English Canada" Speaks Out,* ed. J.L. Granatstein and Kenneth McNaught (Toronto: Doubleday Canada, 1991); Kenneth McRoberts, ed., *Beyond Quebec: Taking Stock of Canada* (Montreal and Kingston: McGill-Queen's University Press, 1995); Michael Ignatieff, *The Rights Revolution* (Toronto: Anansi, 2000).
4 Ignatieff, *Rights Revolution,* 119, emphasis added.
5 Slavoj Žižek, "Multiculturalism, or, the Cultural Logic of Multinational Capitalism," *New Left Review* 225 (1997): 28-51.
6 This nationalist line drawing is implied by the title of Richard Gwyn's *Nationalism without Walls: The Unbearable Lightness of Being Canadian* (Toronto: McClelland and Stewart, 1995), ch. 9.
7 Ignatieff, *Rights Revolution,* 124.
8 Ibid., 134.
9 Kymlicka, *Finding Our Way,* 154-5.
10 Ibid., 155.
11 Ibid., 164.

12 Whitaker, "With or without Quebec?" 27.
13 Kymlicka, *Finding Our Way*, 163.
14 For example, a group of eleven academics and writers expressed support for a three-nations view of Canada in "Three Nations in a Delicate State," *Toronto Star*, 4 February 1992, A17.
15 Quoted by Alain-G. Gagnon, "André Laurendeau: The Search for Political Equality and Social Justice," *Quebec Studies* 27 (Spring/Summer 1999): 88.
16 Whitaker, "With or without Quebec?" 19, emphasis added.
17 McRoberts, *Misconceiving Canada*; Laforest, *Trudeau*.
18 Whitaker, "With or without Quebec?" 19.
19 Angus, *Border Within*, 26-7.
20 Kymlicka, *Finding Our Way*, 168.
21 Ibid.
22 Charles Taylor, "Shared and Divergent Values," in *Reconciling the Solitudes: Essays on Canadian Federalism and Nationalism*, ed. Guy Laforest (Montreal and Kingston: McGill-Queen's University Press, 1993), 183.
23 Taylor concludes *The Malaise of Modernity* with a chapter entitled "Against Fragmentation" (Concord, ON: Anansi, 1991). For a discussion of Taylor's concern with fragmentation, see Samuel LaSelva, *The Moral Foundations of Canadian Federalism: Paradoxes, Achievements, and Tragedies of Nationhood* (Montreal and Kingston: McGill-Queen's University Press, 1996), 186.
24 William Connolly argues that while Taylor rejects a strong form of teleological philosophy along the lines of Hegel, "Taylor proceeds from a rhetoric of self-realization within community, through a rhetoric of communal realization, to a rhetoric of progressive attunement to a harmonious direction in being." *Identity/Difference: Democratic Negotiations of Political Paradox* (Ithaca, NY: Cornell University Press, 1991), 89. For further discussion of Taylor's teleological tendencies, see William Corlett, *Community without Unity: A Politics of Derridian Extravagance* (Durham, NC: Duke University Press, 1989), 51-3.
25 Gwyn, *Nationalism without Walls*, ch. 7.
26 Presumably, this is the English Canada of the former Reform Party/Canadian Alliance and author William Gairdner. In his book *The Trouble with Canada: A Citizen Speaks Out*, Gairdner makes an explicit call to unity through homogeneity, noting that he cannot imagine any other solution to the problem of diversity (Toronto: General Paperbacks, 1990), ch. 14.
27 Resnick, *Thinking English Canada*, ch. 12. Richard Gwyn also uses this phrase in *Nationalism without Walls*, ch. 7.
28 Resnick, *Thinking English Canada*, 72-3.

Chapter 6: The Arithmetic of Canadian Citizenship

1 Department of Indian Affairs and Northern Development, *Statement of the Government of Canada on Indian Policy* (Ottawa, 1969), hereafter cited as "White Paper."
2 Most notable here is Sally M. Weaver, *Making Canadian Indian Policy: The Hidden Agenda 1968-1970* (Toronto: University of Toronto Press, 1981); see also Loretta Czernis, *Weaving a Canadian Allegory: Anonymous Writing, Personal Reading* (Waterloo, ON: Wilfrid Laurier University Press, 1994); J.R. Miller, *Skyscrapers Hide the Heavens: A History of Indian-White Relations in Canada*, 3rd ed. (Toronto: University of Toronto Press, 2000), chs. 12 and 13.

3 H.B. Hawthorn and M.A. Tremblay, *A Survey of the Contemporary Indians of Canada: A Report on Economic, Political, Educational Needs and Policies*, vol. 1 (Ottawa: Queen's Printer, 1966), hereafter cited as "Hawthorn Report."
4 Ibid., 6.
5 Ibid., 6-7, emphasis added.
6 Ibid., 18, 7.
7 Ibid., 8, 18, 12. The eighth recommendation goes on to say, "The Indian Affairs Branch has a special responsibility to see that the 'plus' aspects of Indian citizenship are respected."
8 Ibid., 13.
9 See, for example, R.W. Dunning, "The Hawthorn Report," *Canadian Forum*, June 1967, 52-3.
10 Hawthorn Report, 5.
11 Ibid., 17.
12 Ibid., 10.
13 Ibid., 6.
14 The report itself notes that "quite apart from their intention, the effect of implementing the recommendations in the Report, like the effect of the governmental programs now in question, is not neutral towards the maintenance of autonomous Indian societies within the Canadian nation." Instead of encouraging separatism, the report goes to considerable lengths to argue why, in a range of areas, it is in the best interests of Aboriginal people to pursue paths more in line with Canadian norms. The realities of living in a modern industrial society inevitably limit the degree of separateness that Aboriginal people could possibly achieve. A host of modern influences and pressures, such as the judicial sphere, the dominant languages of Canada, and the costs and benefits of waged work, will all have a profound effect on Aboriginal people. Hawthorn Report, 10.
15 Weaver, *Making Canadian Indian Policy*.
16 White Paper, 9.
17 Ibid.
18 Ibid., 5.
19 Ibid., 8.
20 Ibid., 10.
21 Ibid.
22 Alan C. Cairns, "Aboriginal Canadians, Citizenship, and the Constitution," in *Reconfigurations: Canadian Citizenship and Constitutional Change*, ed. Douglas E. Williams (Toronto: McClelland and Stewart, 1995), 244.
23 James Tully, *Strange Multiplicity: Constitutionalism in an Age of Diversity* (Cambridge: Cambridge University Press, 1995), 208.
24 White Paper, 9.
25 Ibid., 9.
26 Ibid., 9, emphasis added.
27 Ibid., 9.
28 Ibid., 5, emphasis added.
29 Ibid., 9.
30 Ibid., 5.
31 Ibid., 6.

32 Indian Chiefs of Alberta, "Citizens Plus," in *The Only Good Indian: Essays by Canadian Indians*, ed. Waubageshig (Toronto: New Press, 1970), 9.
33 Ibid., 19.
34 Ibid., 10.
35 Weaver, *Making Canadian Indian Policy*, 5. Weaver also states that "the White Paper became the single most powerful catalyst of the Indian nationalist movement, launching it into a determined force for nativism – a reaffirmation of a unique cultural heritage and identity" (171).
36 Miller, *Skyscrapers Hide the Heavens*, 232. Finally, according to the Royal Commission on Aboriginal Peoples, "Resistance to assimilation grew weak, but it never died away. In the fourth stage of the relationship, it caught fire and began to grow into a political movement. One stimulus was the federal government's White Paper on Indian policy, issued in 1969." *Report of the Royal Commission on Aboriginal Peoples* (Ottawa: Canada Communications Group, 1996), ch. 1, <www.ainc-inac.gc.ca/ch/rcap/rpt/> (12 April 2005).
37 Pierre Elliott Trudeau, *Conversations with Canadians* (Toronto: University of Toronto Press, 1972).
38 Mary Ellen Turpel, "The Charlottetown Discord and Aboriginal Peoples' Struggles for Fundamental Political Change," in *The Charlottetown Accord, the Referendum, and the Future of Canada*, ed. Kenneth McRoberts and Patrick Monahan (Toronto: University of Toronto Press, 1993), 137.
39 Indian Chiefs of Alberta, "Citizens Plus," 12.
40 Douglas Sanders, "The Renewal of Indian Special Status," in *Equality Rights and the Canadian Charter of Rights and Freedoms*, ed. Ann F. Bayefsky and Mary Eberts (Toronto: Carswell, 1985), 560.
41 *The National*, CBC, 11 October 1992, placement 11. Placements indicate the order of the item in the newscast.
42 *CTV News*, 7 October 1992, placement 1.
43 *The Journal*, CBC, 5 October 1992, placement 1.
44 For an interesting discussion of a somewhat similar tendency to use inversion in the United States, see Ronald Dworkin, *Taking Rights Seriously* (Cambridge, MA: Harvard University Press, 1977), 229.
45 Turpel, "Charlottetown Discord," 138.
46 Chrétien quoted in Shawn Ohler, "Different and Equal," *National Post*, 2 April 1999, <www.nationalpst.com/news> (2 April 1999).
47 Beverley McLachlin, "The Civilization of Difference." Fourth Annual Lafontaine-Baldwin Lecture, Halifax, March 2003. <www.operation-dialogue.com/lafontaine-baldwin> (4 November 2004).
48 Alan Cairns, *Citizens Plus: Aboriginal Peoples and the Canadian State* (Vancouver: UBC Press, 2000); Will Kymlicka, *Finding Our Way: Rethinking Ethnocultural Relations in Canada* (Toronto: Oxford University Press, 1998); James Tully, *Strange Multiplicity: Constitutionalism in an Age of Diversity* (Cambridge: Cambridge University Press, 1995).
49 Tom Flanagan, *First Nations? Second Thoughts* (Montreal and Kingston: McGill-Queen's University Press, 2000).
50 Alan C. Cairns and Tom Flanagan, "An Exchange," *Inroads: The Canadian Journal of Opinion* 10 (2001): 101-22.

51 Ibid., 112.
52 Cairns, *Citizens Plus*.

Chapter 7: Misrepresenting the Canadian Conversation

1 Simone Chambers, "New Constitutionalism: Democracy, Habermas, and Canadian Exceptionalism," in *Canadian Political Philosophy: Contemporary Reflections*, ed. Ronald Beiner and Wayne Norman (Toronto: Oxford University Press, 2001), 65.
2 Michael Ignatieff, *The Rights Revolution* (Toronto: Anansi, 2000), 7.
3 Canada, Charlottetown Accord, draft legal text (Ottawa: Ministry of Supply and Services, 9 October 1992).
4 *CTV News*, 17 September 1992, placement 8; Ian Hanomansingh, *The National*, CBC, 18 September 1992, placement 5. Placements indicate the order of the item in the newscast.
5 *The Journal*, CBC, 10 September 1992, placement 3.
6 *The Journal*, CBC, 8 October 1992, placement 4.
7 *The Journal*, CBC, 3 September 1992, placement 1.
8 *The National*, CBC, 9 September 1992, placement 3.
9 *The National*, CBC, 19 October 1992, placement 4.
10 *The Journal*, CBC, 13 October 1992, placement 1.
11 *The Journal*, CBC, 12 October 1992, placement 1.
12 *The National*, CBC, 13 October 1992, placement 3.
13 *Sunday Report*, CBC, 18 October 1992, placement 10.
14 *The National*, CBC, 9 October 1992, placement 2. A similar report aired on *CTV News*, 9 October 1992, placement 3.
15 Chambers, "New Constitutionalism," 64.
16 National Media Archives, *National Referendum Summary Data*.
17 Martha Minow, *Making All the Difference: Inclusion, Exclusion, and American Law* (Ithaca, NY: Cornell University Press, 1990).
18 Lloyd Robertson, *CTV News*, 13 October 1992, placement 6; *The National*, CBC, 13 October 1992, placement 3.
19 Most of these groups were active on the "yes" side and were created specifically to take part in the referendum campaign. One of these was introduced thus: "They call themselves 'Women for the YES' but these aren't just any women. They're political wives: Mila Mulroney, Andrée Bourassa, and Aline Chrétien." Tonda MacCharles, *The National*, CBC, 15 October 1992, placement 2. Other women's groups of a more permanent nature also expressed their views on the accord, including a group representing Quebec businesswomen and the National Federation of French Canadian Women Outside of Quebec.
20 *Sunday Report*, CBC, 14 September 1992, placement 2.
21 *CTV News*, 27 September 1992, placement 7.
22 *CTV News*, 15 September 1992, placement 5.
23 *CTV News*, 4 October 1992, placement 6.
24 Samuel LaSelva, *The Moral Foundations of Canadian Federalism: Paradoxes, Achievements, and Tragedies of Nationhood* (Montreal and Kingston: McGill-Queen's University Press, 1996), 169. LaSelva's alternative route to dealing with diversity is a renewed fraternity.

25 Alan Cairns, "The Fragmentation of Canadian Citizenship," in *Reconfigurations: Canadian Citizenship and Constitutional Change*, ed. Douglas E. Williams (Toronto: McClelland and Stewart, 1995), 175-6.
26 Will Kymlicka, "The New Debate over Minority Rights," in *Canadian Political Philosophy*, ed. Ronald Beiner and Wayne Norman (Toronto: Oxford University Press, 2001), 81 (endnotes omitted).
27 Chambers, "New Constitutionalism."
28 Linda Trimble, "'Good Enough Citizens': Canadian Women and Representation in Constitutional Deliberations," *International Journal of Canadian Studies* 17 (Spring 1998): 131-56.

Chapter 8: Civil Eyes

1 Personal communication, Hamilton, Ontario, 4 February 1998.
2 "The 'Canadian' Diversity Model: Making it Work," Canadian Policy Research Network, roundtable discussion, Ottawa, 17 September 2001.
3 Kenneth McRae, ed., *Consociational Democracy: Political Accommodation in Segmented Societies* (Toronto: McClelland and Stewart, 1974).
4 Will Kymlicka, *Multicultural Citizenship: A Liberal Theory of Minority Rights* (Oxford: Oxford University Press, 1995).
5 See, for example, Brian Barry, *Culture and Equality: An Egalitarian Critique of Multiculturalism* (Cambridge, MA: Harvard University Press, 1999); Joseph Carens, *Culture, Citizenship, and Community: A Contextual Exploration of Justice As Evenhandedness* (Oxford: Oxford University Press, 2000).
6 Will Kymlicka, "The New Debate over Minority Rights," in *Canadian Political Philosophy: Contemporary Reflections*, ed. Ronald Beiner and Wayne Norman (Toronto: Oxford University Press, 2001), 169. Presumably, Brian Barry would disagree with Kymlicka that the "old" multiculturalism debate is over. Brian Barry, *Culture and Equality: An Egalitarian Critique of Multiculturalism* (Cambridge, MA: Harvard University Press, 1999).
7 House of Commons, Debates, 8 October 1971, 8545-8.
8 Bibby, *Mosaic Madness: The Poverty and Potential of Life in Canada* (Toronto: Stoddart, 1990); Neil Bissondath, *Selling Illusions: The Cult of Multiculturalism in Canada* (Toronto: Penguin, 1994); Richard Gwyn, *Nationalism without Walls: The Unbearable Lightness of Being Canadian* (Toronto: McClelland and Stewart, 1995).
9 Neil Bissoondath, *Selling Illusions*, 143.
10 Will Kymlicka, *Finding Our Way: Rethinking Ethnocultural Relations in Canada* (Toronto: Oxford University Press, 1998), 61.
11 Taylor, "The Politics of Recognition," 64.
12 Ibid., 66.
13 Ibid., 64.
14 Ibid., 73.
15 Ibid., 66, emphasis added.
16 Homi K. Bhabha, "Culture's in Between," in *Multicultural States: Rethinking Difference and Identity*, ed. David Bennett (London: Routledge, 1998), 32-3.
17 For a somewhat sympathetic critique of Taylor on this question, see Ian Angus, *A Border Within: National Identity, Cultural Plurality, and Wilderness* (Montreal and

Kingston: McGill-Queen's University Press, 1997), 151-4. Lorraine Code draws on Gadamer to some degree, suggesting that "the potentially engulfing, merging potential of a fusion of horizons is not unequivocally desirable, and Gadamer does not take power into account, either as a given or as a goal." *What Can She Know?* (Ithaca, NY: Cornell University Press, 1991), 201. She goes on to draw from Foucault as a corrective to these flaws.

18 Bhabha, "Culture's in Between," 30.
19 This concept is examined by Lorraine Code in *Epistemic Responsibility* (Hanover, NH: University Press of New England, 1987) and in *What Can She Know?*
20 Michel Foucault, *Discipline and Punish: The Birth of the Prison*, trans. Alan Sheridan (New York: Vintage Books, 1979). See, in particular, part 3, chapter 3. Foucault elaborated on his use of panopticism in an interview with Jean-Pierre Barou and Michelle Perrot, "The Eye of Power," in *Power/Knowledge: Selected Interviews and Other Writings 1972-1977*, ed. Colin Gordon (New York: Pantheon, 1980).
21 Foucault, *Discipline and Punish*, 204.
22 The phrase "multicultural panopticon" has been used in a different context by Reg Whitaker. His usage centres on the relationship between new information technologies and consumer capitalism and the ways in which certain identities are differentiated and fragmented even as they are unified into global capitalism. *The End of Privacy: How Total Surveillance Is Becoming a Reality* (New York: The New Press, 1999), chapter 6.
23 Steven Mann, Jason Nolan, and Barry Wellman, "Sousveillance: Inventing and Using Wearable Computing Devices for Data Collection in Surveillance Environments," *Surveillance and Society* 1(3): 338.
24 Mann, Nolan, and Wellman, "Sousveillance," 347.
25 Michel Foucault, "Governmentality," in *The Foucault Effect: Studies in Governmentality*, ed. Graham Burchell, Colin Gordon, and Peter Miller (Chicago: University of Chicago Press, 1991).
26 For example, see Andrew Barry, Thomas Osborne, and Nikolas Rose, *Foucault and Political Reason* (Chicago: University of Chicago Press, 1996); Kirstie M. McClure, "Taking Liberties in Foucault's Triangle; Sovereignty, Discipline, Governmentality, and the Subject of Rights," in *Identities, Politics, and Rights*, ed. Austin Sarat and Thomas R. Kearns (Ann Arbor: University of Michigan Press, 1997).
27 As quoted in Barry Hindess, *Discourses of Power: From Hobbes to Foucault* (Oxford, Blackwell Publishers, 1996), 99.
28 Foucault, "Governmentality," 100.
29 While she understands his lectures on governmentality to be something of an exception, Wendy Brown criticizes Foucault for not focusing enough attention on the bureaucratic state itself, as well as capitalist modes of production, in producing subjects. *States of Injury: Power and Freedom in Late Modernity* (Princeton: Princeton University Press, 1995).
30 Foucault, "Governmentality," 102.
31 Colin Gordon, "Governmental Rationality: An Introduction," in *The Foucault Effect*, 5.
32 Hindess, *Discourses of Power*, 130. See also Gordon, "Governmental Rationality," 47.

33 Louis Althusser, "Ideology and Ideological State Apparatuses (Notes towards an Investigation)," in *Lenin and Philosophy and Other Essays*, trans. Ben Brewster (New York: Monthly Review Press, 1971); Judith Butler, *The Psychic Life of Power* (Stanford: Stanford University Press, 1997), chapters 3 and 4.
34 Bhiku C. Parekh, *Rethinking Multiculturalism: Cultural Diversity and Political Theory* (Cambridge, MA: Harvard University Press, 2000), 230.
35 CBC, *Culture Shock*, episodes aired on 23 October, 20 November, and 27 November 1999. Descriptions accessed from <www.cbc.ca> on 18 December 1999.

Chapter 9: There's No Place Like Home

1 Charles Taylor, *The Malaise of Modernity* (Concord, ON: Anansi, 1991); Will Kymlicka, *Finding Our Way: Rethinking Ethnocultural Relations in Canada* (Toronto: Oxford University Press, 1998); Will Kymlicka, *Multicultural Citizenship: A Liberal Theory of Minority Rights* (Oxford: Oxford University Press, 1995).
2 James Tully, "Diversity's Gambit Declined," in *Constitutional Predicament: Canada after the Referendum of 1992*, ed. Curtis Cook (Montreal and Kingston: McGill-Queen's University Press, 1994).

Bibliography

Abbey, Ruth. *Charles Taylor*. Princeton: Princeton University Press, 2000.
Abu-Laban, Yasmeen, and Christina Gabriel. *Selling Diversity: Immigration, Multiculturalism, Employment Equity, and Globalization*. Peterborough, ON: Broadview Press, 2002.
Ajzenstat, Janet. "Decline of Procedural Liberalism: The Slippery Slope to Secession." In *Is Quebec Nationalism Just? Perspectives from Anglophone Canada*, ed. Joseph H. Carens, 120-36. Montreal and Kingston: McGill-Queen's University Press, 1995.
–. "Liberalism and Assimilation: Lord Durham Reconsidered." In *Political Thought in Canada*, ed. Stephen Brooks, 239-57. Toronto: Irwin Publishing, 1984.
–. *The Political Thought of Lord Durham*. Montreal and Kingston: McGill-Queen's University Press, 1988.
Ajzenstat, Janet, and Peter Smith, eds. *Canada's Origins: Liberal, Tory, or Republican?* 1-18. Ottawa: Carleton University Press, 1995.
Alfred, Taiaiake. *Peace, Power, Righteousness: An Indigenous Manifesto*. Toronto: Oxford University Press, 1999.
Althusser, Louis. "Ideology and Ideological State Apparatuses (Notes towards an Investigation)." In *Lenin and Philosophy and Other Essays,* trans. Ben Brewster. New York: Monthly Review Press, 1971.
Anderson, Benedict. *Imagined Communities: Reflections on the Origin and Spread of Nationalism*. London: Verso, 1983.
Anderssen, Erin, and Michael Valpy. *The New Canada: A Globe and Mail Report on the Next Generation*. Toronto: McClelland and Stewart, 2004.
Angus, Ian. *A Border Within: National Identity, Cultural Plurality, and Wilderness*. Montreal and Kingston: McGill-Queen's University Press, 1997.
Bakan, Joel. *Just Words: Constitutional Rights, Social Wrongs*. Toronto: University of Toronto Press, 1997.
Balthazar, Louis. "Identity and Nationalism in Quebec." In *Clash of Identities: Essays on Media, Manipulation, and Politics of the Self*, ed. James Littleton, 101-12. Toronto: Prentice Hall, 1996.
Bannerji, Himani. *The Dark Side of the Nation: Essays on Multiculturalism, Nationalism and Gender*. Toronto: Canadian Scholars' Press, 2000.
Barry, Andrew, Thomas Osborne, and Nikolas Rose. *Foucault and Political Reason*. Chicago: University of Chicago Press, 1996.
Barry, Brian. *Culture and Equality: An Egalitarian Critique of Multiculturalism*. Cambridge, MA: Harvard University Press, 1999.

Behiels, Michael, ed. *The Meech Lake Primer: Conflicting Views of the 1987 Constitutional Accord.* Ottawa: University of Ottawa Press, 1989.
Beiner, Ronald, ed. *Theorizing Nationalism.* Albany: SUNY Press, 1999.
Beiner, Ronald, and Wayne Norman, eds. *Canadian Political Philosophy: Contemporary Reflections.* Toronto: Oxford University Press, 2001.
Bell, David V.J. *The Roots of Disunity: A Study of Canadian Political Culture.* Rev. ed. Toronto: Oxford University Press, 1992.
Benhabib, Seyla. *The Claims of Culture: Equality and Diversity in the Global Era.* Princeton, NJ: Princeton University Press, 2002.
Bennett, David, ed. *Multicultural States: Rethinking Difference and Identity.* London: Routledge, 1998.
Bercuson, David, and Barry Cooper. *Deconfederation: Canada without Quebec.* Toronto: Key Porter Books, 1991.
Berger, Thomas. "Quebec's Rendezvous with Independence." In *"English Canada" Speaks Out,* ed. J.L. Granatstein and Kenneth McNaught. Toronto: Doubleday Canada, 1991.
Bhabha, Homi K. "Culture's in Between." In *Multicultural States: Rethinking Difference and Identity,* ed. David Bennett. London: Routledge, 1998.
–. *The Location of Culture.* London: Routledge, 1994.
–, ed. *Nation and Narration.* London: Routledge, 1990.
Bibby, Reginald W. *Mosaic Madness: The Poverty and Potential of Life in Canada.* Toronto: Stoddart, 1990.
Bissoondath, Neil. *Selling Illusions: The Cult of Multiculturalism in Canada.* Toronto: Penguin, 1994.
Blattberg, Charles. *Shall We Dance? A Patriotic Politics for Canada.* Montreal and Kingston: McGill-Queen's University Press, 2003.
Bock, Gisela, and Susan James, eds. *Beyond Equality and Difference: Citizenship, Feminist Politics and Female Subjectivity.* London: Routledge, 1992.
Brown, Wendy. *States of Injury: Power and Freedom in Late Modernity.* Princeton: Princeton University Press, 1995.
Brubaker, Rogers. "Myths and Misconceptions in the Study of Nationalism." In *National Self-Determinism and Secession,* ed. Margaret Moore, 233-65. Oxford: Oxford University Press, 1998.
–. *Nationalism Reframed: Nationhood and the National Question in the New Europe.* Cambridge: Cambridge University Press, 1996.
Butler, Judith. *Gender Trouble: Feminism and the Subversion of Identity.* New York: Routledge, Chapman and Hall, 1990.
–. "Merely Cultural." *New Left Review* 227 (1998): 33-44.
–. *The Psychic Life of Power.* Stanford: Stanford University Press, 1997.
Butler, Judith, Ernesto Laclau, and Slavoj Žižek. *Contingency, Hegemony, Universality: Contemporary Dialogues on the Left.* London: Verso, 2000.
Cairns, Alan C. *Citizens Plus: Aboriginal Peoples and the Canadian State.* Vancouver: UBC Press, 2000.
–. *Disruptions: Constitutional Struggles, from the Charter to Meech Lake,* ed. Douglas E. Williams. Toronto: McClelland and Stewart, 1991.
–. *Reconfigurations: Canadian Citizenship and Constitutional Change,* ed. Douglas E. Williams. Toronto: McClelland and Stewart, 1995.
Cairns, Alan C., and Tom Flanagan. "An Exchange." *Inroads: The Canadian Journal of Opinion* 10 (2001): 101-22.

Bibliography

Cameron, David. "Lord Durham Then and Now." *Journal of Canadian Studies* 25 (Spring 1990): 5-23.

Canada. Highlights from the Royal Commission on Aboriginal Peoples. Ottawa: Canada Communications Group, 1996.

Cardinal, Harold. *The Unjust Society: The Tragedy of Canada's Indians*. Edmonton: Hurtig Publishing, 1969.

Carens, Joseph. *Culture, Citizenship, and Community: A Contextual Exploration of Justice As Evenhandedness*. Oxford: Oxford University Press, 2000.

–. "Dimensions of Citizenship and National Identity in Canada." *Philosophical Forum* 28, 1-2 (1997): 111-24.

–, ed. *Is Quebec Nationalism Just? Perspectives from Anglophone Canada*. Montreal and Kingston: McGill-Queen's University Press, 1995.

Chambers, Simone. "New Constitutionalism: Democracy, Habermas, and Canadian Exceptionalism." In *Canadian Political Philosophy: Contemporary Reflections*, ed. Ronald Beiner and Wayne Norman, 63-77. Toronto: Oxford University Press, 2001.

Charlton, Mark, and Paul Barker, eds. *Crosscurrents: Contemporary Political Issues*. 4th ed. Toronto: Nelson, 2002.

Code, Lorraine. *What Can She Know?* Ithaca, NY: Cornell University Press, 1991.

Connolly, William. *The Ethos of Pluralization*. Minneapolis: University of Minnesota Press, 1995.

–. *Identity/Difference: Democratic Negotiations of Political Paradox*. Ithaca, NY: Cornell University Press, 1991.

Cook, Ramsay. *Canada and the French-Canadian Question*. Toronto: Macmillan, 1966.

–. *Canada, Québec and the Uses of Nationalism*. 2nd ed. Toronto: McClelland and Stewart, 1995.

Corlett, William. *Community without Unity: A Politics of Derridian Extravagance*. Durham, NC: Duke University Press, 1989.

Couture, Claude. *Paddling with the Current: Pierre Elliott Trudeau, Étienne Parent, Liberalism and Nationalism in Canada*, trans. Vivien Bosley. Edmonton: University of Alberta Press, 1998.

Craig, G.M., ed. *An Abridgement of the Report on the Affairs of British North America by Lord Durham*. Ottawa: Carleton University Press, 1982.

Czernis, Loretta. *Weaving a Canadian Allegory: Anonymous Writing, Personal Reading*. Waterloo, ON: Wilfrid Laurier University Press, 1994.

Day, Richard J.F. *Multiculturalism and the History of Canadian Diversity*. Toronto: University of Toronto Press, 2000.

Denis, Claude. *We Are Not You: First Nations and Canadian Modernity*. Peterborough, ON: Broadview, 1997.

Department of Indian Affairs and Northern Development. *Statement of the Government of Canada on Indian Policy*. White paper. Ottawa, 1969.

Dworkin, Ronald. *Taking Rights Seriously*. Cambridge, MA: Harvard University Press, 1977.

Eisenberg, Avigail. "Domination and Political Representation in Canada." In *Painting the Maple: Essays on Race, Gender, and the Construction of Canada*, ed. Veronica Strong-Boag, Sherill Grace, Avigail Eisenberg, and Joan Anderson. Vancouver: UBC Press, 1998.

Flanagan, Tom. *First Nations? Second Thoughts*. Montreal and Kingston: McGill-Queen's University Press, 2000.

Bibliography

Flax, Jane. "Beyond Equality and Difference: Gender, Justice and Difference." In *Beyond Equality and Difference: Citizenship, Feminist Politics and Female Subjectivity*, ed. Gisela Bock and Susan James. London: Routledge, 1992.

Forbes, Donald. "Hartz/Horowitz at Twenty: Nationalism, Toryism and Socialism in Canada and the United States." *Canadian Journal of Political Science* 20, 2 (1987): 287-315.

Foucault, Michel. *Discipline and Punish: The Birth of the Prison*, trans. Alan Sheridan. New York: Vintage Books, 1979.

–. "The Eye of Power." Interview by Jean-Pierre Barou and Michelle Perrot. In *Power/Knowledge: Selected Interviews and Other Writings 1972-1977*, ed. Colin Gordon. New York: Pantheon, 1980.

–. "Governmentality." In *The Foucault Effect: Studies in Governmentality*, ed. Graham Burchell, Colin Gordon, and Peter Miller. Chicago: University of Chicago Press, 1991.

Fraser, Nancy. "Heterosexism, Misrecognition and Capitalism: A Response to Judith Butler." *New Left Review* 228 (1998): 140-9.

–. *Justice Interruptus: Critical Reflections on the "Postsocialist" Condition*. New York: Routledge, 1997.

–. "A Rejoinder to Iris Young." *New Left Review* 223 (1997): 126-9.

Gagnon, Alain-G. "André Laurendeau: The Search for Political Equality and Social Justice." *Quebec Studies* 27 (Spring/Summer 1999): 42-5.

Gagnon, Christiane. "Bloc Quebecois: Integration Rather Than Multiculturalism." In *The Battle over Multiculturalism: Does It Help or Hinder Canadian Unity?* ed. Andrew Cardozo and Louis Musto, vol. 1. Ottawa: PSI Publishing, 1997.

Gairdner, William. *The Trouble with Canada: A Citizen Speaks Out*. Toronto: General Paperbacks, 1990.

Gitlin, Tod. *The Twilight of Common Dreams: Why America Is Wracked by Culture Wars*. New York: Henry Holt and Company, 1995.

Goldie, Terry, ed. *In a Queer Country: Gay and Lesbian Studies in the Canadian Context*. Vancouver: Arsenal Pulp Press, 2001.

Gordon, Colin. "Governmental Rationality: An Introduction." In *The Foucault Effect: Studies in Governmentality*, ed. Graham Burchell, Colin Gordon, and Peter Miller. Chicago: University of Chicago Press, 1991.

Gutmann, Amy. *Identity in Democracy*. Princeton, NJ: Princeton University Press, 2004.

Gwyn, Richard. *Nationalism without Walls: The Unbearable Lightness of Being Canadian*. Toronto: McClelland and Stewart, 1995.

Habermas, Jürgen. "The European Nation-State: On the Past and Future of Sovereignty and Citizenship." In *The Inclusion of the Other: Studies in Political Theory*, ed. Ciaran Cronin and Pablo DeGreiff. Cambridge, MA: MIT Press, 1998.

Hartney, Michael. "Some Confusions Concerning Collective Rights." In *The Rights of Minority Cultures*, ed. Will Kymlicka. Oxford: Oxford University Press, 1995.

Hawthorn, H.B., and M.A. Tremblay. *A Survey of the Contemporary Indians of Canada: A Report on Economic, Political, Educational Needs and Policies*. Ottawa: Queen's Printers, 1966.

Honig, Bonnie. *Democracy and the Foreigner*. Princeton: Princeton University Press, 2001.

–. "Difference, Dilemmas and the Politics of Home." In *Democracy and Difference: Contesting the Boundaries of the Political*, ed. Seyla Benhabib. Princeton: Princeton University Press, 1996.

Bibliography

Horowitz, Gad. "Conservatism, Liberalism, and Socialism in Canada: An Interpretation." *Canadian Journal of Economic and Political Science* 32 (May 1966): 143-71.
—. "Creative Politics, Mosaics, and Identity." In *Everybody's Canada: The Vertical Mosaic Reviewed and Re-examined,* ed. James L. Heap. Don Mills, ON: Burns and MacEachern, 1974.
—. "Notes on Conservatism, Liberalism and Socialism in Canada." *Canadian Journal of Political Science* 11, 2 (1978): 383-99.
—. "Toward the Democratic Class Struggle." In *Agenda 1970: Proposals for a Creative Politics,* ed. Trevor Lloyd and Jack McLeod. Toronto: University of Toronto Press, 1968.
Ignatieff, Michael. *Blood and Belonging: Journeys into the New Nationalism.* Toronto: Penguin Books, 1993.
—. *The Rights Revolution.* Toronto: Anansi, 2000.
Indian Chiefs of Alberta. "Citizens Plus." In *The Only Good Indian: Essays by Canadian Indians,* ed. Waubageshig. Toronto: New Press, 1970.
Iyer, Pico. "Imagining Canada: An Outsider's Hope for a Global Future." Inaugural Hart House Lecture, Toronto, 5 April 2001.
Jakobsen, Janet R. *Working Alliances and the Politics of Difference: Diversity and Feminist Ethics.* Bloomington: Indiana University Press, 1998.
Johnston, Darlene M. "Native Rights As Collective Rights: A Question of Group Self-Preservation." In *The Rights of Minority Cultures,* ed. Will Kymlicka. Oxford: Oxford University Press, 1995.
Johnston, Donald, ed. *With a Bang, Not a Whimper: Pierre Trudeau Speaks Out.* Toronto: Stoddart, 1988.
Keohane, Kieran. *Symptoms of Canada: An Essay on the Canadian Identity.* Toronto: University of Toronto Press, 1997.
Knopff, Rainer, and F.L. Morton. "Canada's Court Party." In *Rethinking the Constitution: Perspectives on Canadian Constitutional Reform, Interpretation, and Theory,* ed. Anthony A. Peacock. Toronto: Oxford University Press, 1996.
—. *Charter Politics.* Toronto: Nelson Canada, 1992.
Kymlicka, Will. *Finding Our Way: Rethinking Ethnocultural Relations in Canada.* Toronto: Oxford University Press, 1998.
—. *Liberalism, Community and Culture.* Oxford: Oxford University Press, 1989.
—. *Multicultural Citizenship: A Liberal Theory of Minority Rights.* Oxford: Oxford University Press, 1995.
—. "The New Debate over Minority Rights." In *Canadian Political Philosophy: Contemporary Reflections,* ed. Ronald Beiner and Wayne Norman. Toronto: Oxford University Press, 2001.
—. "Three Forms of Group Differentiated Citizenship in Canada." In *Democracy and Difference: Contesting the Boundaries of the Political,* ed. Seyla Benhabib. Princeton: Princeton University Press, 1996.
Kymlicka, Will, and Wayne Norman. "Return of the Citizen: A Survey of Recent Work on Citizenship Theory." In *Theorizing Citizenship,* ed. Ronald Beiner. Albany: SUNY Press, 1995.
Laforest, Guy. "Philosophy and Political Judgment in a Multinational Federation." In *Philosophy in an Age of Pluralism: The Philosophy of Charles Taylor in Question,* ed. James Tully. Cambridge: Cambridge University Press, 1994.
—. *Trudeau and the End of a Canadian Dream,* trans. Paul Leduc Browne and Michelle Weinroth. Montreal and Kingston: McGill-Queen's University Press, 1995.

Bibliography

LaSelva, Samuel. *The Moral Foundations of Canadian Federalism: Paradoxes, Achievements, and Tragedies of Nationhood.* Montreal and Kingston: McGill-Queen's University Press, 1996.
Lee, Jo-Anne, and Linda Cardinal. "Hegemonic Nationalism and the Politics of Feminism in Canada." In *Painting the Maple: Essays on Race, Gender, and the Construction of Canada,* ed. Veronica Strong-Boag, Sherrill Grace, Avigail Eisenberg, and Joan Anderson, 215-41. Vancouver: UBC Press, 1998.
Mackey, Eva. *The House of Difference: Cultural Politics and National Identity in Canada.* London: Routledge, 1999.
McLachlin, Beverley. "The Civilization of Difference." Fourth Annual Lafontaine-Baldwin Lecture, Halifax, 7 March 2003. <www.operation-dialogue.com/lafontaine-baldwin> (4 November 2004).
Maclure, Jocelyn. *Quebec Identity: The Challenge of Pluralism,* trans. Peter Feldstein. Montreal and Kingston: McGill-Queen's University Press, 2003.
McClure, Kirstie M. "Taking Liberties in Foucault's Triangle: Sovereignty, Discipline, Governmentality, and the Subject of Rights." In *Identities, Politics, and Rights,* ed. Austin Sarat and Thomas R. Kearns. Ann Arbor: University of Michigan Press, 1997.
McRoberts, Kenneth. *Misconceiving Canada: The Struggle for National Unity.* Toronto: Oxford University Press, 1997.
–, ed. *Beyond Quebec: Taking Stock of Canada.* Montreal and Kingston: McGill-Queen's University Press, 1995.
McRoberts, Kenneth, and Patrick Monahan, eds. *The Charlottetown Accord, the Referendum, and the Future of Canada.* Toronto: University of Toronto Press, 1993.
Maillé, Chantal. "Québec Women and the Constitutional Issue: A Scattered Group." *Journal of Canadian Studies* 35, 2 (2000).
Mandel, Michael. *The Charter of Rights and the Legalization of Politics in Canada.* Rev. ed. Toronto: Thompson Educational Publishing, 1994.
Mann, Steven, Jason Nolan, and Barry Wellman. "Sousveillance: Inventing and Using Wearable Computing Devices for Data Collection in Surveillance Environments," *Surveillance and Society* 1 (3): 338.
Miller, J.R. *Skyscrapers Hide the Heavens: A History of Indian-White Relations in Canada.* 3rd ed. Toronto: University of Toronto Press, 2000.
–. "Unity/Diversity: The Canadian Experience: From Confederation to the First World War." In *Readings in Canadian History: Post-Confederation,* ed. R. Douglas Francis and Donald B. Smith. 4th ed. Toronto: Harcourt and Brace and Company Canada, 1994.
Milne, David. "Equality or Asymmetry: Why Choose?" In *Options for a New Canada,* ed. Ronald L. Watts and Douglas M. Brown, 285-307. Toronto: University of Toronto Press, 1991.
Minow, Martha. *Making All the Difference: Inclusion, Exclusion, and American Law.* Ithaca, NY: Cornell University Press, 1990.
Monahan, Patrick J. *Meech Lake: The Inside Story.* Toronto: University of Toronto Press, 1991.
Monture-Angus, Patricia. *Journeying Forward: Dreaming First Nations' Independence.* Halifax: Fernwood, 1999.
Moodley, Kogila. "Canadian Multiculturalism As Ideology." *Ethnic and Racial Studies* 6, 3 (1983): 320-31.
Morton, F.L., and Rainer Knopff. *The Charter Revolution and the Court Party.* Peterborough, ON: Broadview, 2000.

Bibliography

National Action Committee on the Status of Women. "NAC says 'NO': The Charlottetown Agreement Threatens Equality Rights." Toronto, 1992.

–. "NAC's Response to the Report of the Special Joint Committee on 'A Renewed Canada' (Beaudoin-Dobbie)." Toronto, May 1992.

Nicholson, Linda. "To Be or Not to Be: Charles Taylor on the Politics of Recognition." *Constellations* 3, 1 (1996): 1-16.

Pal, Leslie. *Interests of State: The Politics of Language, Multiculturalism, and Feminism in Canada*. Montreal and Kingston: McGill-Queen's University Press, 1993.

Parekh, Bhiku C. *Rethinking Multiculturalism: Cultural Diversity and Political Theory*. Cambridge, MA: Harvard University Press, 2000.

Rankin, Pauline. "Sexualities and National Identities: Re-imagining Queer Nationalism." *Journal of Canadian Studies* 35, 2 (2000): 176-96.

Rawls, John. *A Theory of Justice*. Cambridge, MA: Belknap Press of Harvard University Press, 1971.

Razack, Sherene H. *Canadian Feminism and the Law: The Women's Legal Education and Action Fund and the Pursuit of Equality*. Toronto: Second Story Press, 1991.

–. *Looking White People in the Eye*. Toronto: University of Toronto Press, 1998.

Rémillard, Gil. "Quebec's Quest for Survival and Equality via the Meech Lake Accord." In *The Meech Lake Primer: Conflicting Views of the 1987 Constitutional Accord*, ed. Michael Behiels. Ottawa: University of Ottawa Press, 1989.

Resnick, Philip. *The Politics of Resentment: British Columbia Regionalism and Canadian Unity*. Vancouver: UBC Press, 2000.

–. *Thinking English Canada*. Toronto: Stoddart, 1994.

Richler, Mordecai. *Oh Canada! Oh Quebec! Requiem for a Divided Country*. Toronto: Penguin, 1992.

Ross, Becki. "A Lesbian Politics of Erotic Decolonization." In *Painting the Maple: Essays on Race, Gender and the Construction of Canada*, ed. Veronica Strong-Boag, Sherrill Grace, Avigail Eisenberg, and Joan Anderson. Vancouver: UBC Press, 1998.

Royal Commission on Bilingualism and Biculturalism. *Report of the Royal Commission on Bilingualism and Biculturalism*. Book 4, *The Cultural Contribution of the Other Ethnic Groups*. Ottawa: Queen's Printer, 1970.

Russell, Peter H. *Constitutional Odyssey: Can Canadians Become a Sovereign People?* Toronto: University of Toronto Press, 2004.

–. "The Political Purposes of the Canadian Charter of Rights and Freedoms." *Canadian Bar Review* 61 (1983): 30-54.

Salée, Daniel. "Identities in Conflict: The Aboriginal Question and the Politics of Recognition in Quebec." *Ethnic and Racial Studies* 18, 2 (1995): 277-314.

Sanders, Douglas. "The Renewal of Indian Special Status." In *Equality Rights and the Canadian Charter of Rights and Freedoms*, ed. Anne Bayefsky and Mary Eberts. Toronto: Carswell, 1985.

Schlesinger, Arthur M., Jr. *The Disuniting of America: Reflections on a Multicultural Society*. Rev. ed. New York: W.W. Norton and Company, 1998.

Schwartz, Brian. "Canada Cannot Be Held Together by Taking It Apart." In *"English Canada" Speaks Out*, ed. J.L. Granatstein and Kenneth McNaught, 335-48. Toronto: Doubleday Canada, 1991.

Scott, Joan W. "Deconstructing Equality-Versus-Difference: Or, the Uses of Poststructuralist Theory for Feminism." In *Conflicts in Feminism*, ed. Marianne Hirsch and Evelyn Fox Keller. New York: Routledge, 1990.

–. *Gender and the Politics of History.* New York: Columbia University Press, 1988.
–. "Multiculturalism and the Politics of Identity." *October* 61 (1992): 12-19.
Sigurdson, Richard. "Left- and Right-Wing Charterphobia in Canada: A Critique of the Critics." *International Journal of Canadian Studies* 7-8 (1993): 95-115.
Simeon, Richard, and Mary Janigan, eds. *Toolkits and Building Blocks: Constructing a New Canada.* Toronto: C.D. Howe Institute, 1991.
Smiley, Donald. *Canada in Question: Federalism in the Seventies.* 2nd ed. Toronto: McGraw-Hill Ryerson, 1976.
Smith, Allan. "Metaphor and Nationality in North America." *Canadian Historical Review* 51, 3 (1970): 247-75.
Smith, Nicholas H. *Charles Taylor: Meaning, Morals, and Modernity.* Malden, MA: Polity Press, 2002.
Sniderman, Paul M., Joseph F. Fletcher, Peter H. Russell, and Philip E. Tetlock. *The Clash of Rights: Liberty, Equality, and Legitimacy in Pluralist Democracy.* New Haven: Yale University Press, 1996.
Stasiulis, Daiva. "'Deep Diversity': Race and Ethnicity in Canadian Politics." In *Canadian Politics in the 1990s,* ed. Michael S. Whittington and Glen Williams. 4th ed. Scarborough, ON: Nelson Canada, 1995.
Taylor, Charles. "Alternative Futures: Legitimacy, Identity, and Alienation in Late Twentieth Century Canada." In *Constitutionalism, Citizenship and Society in Canada,* ed. Alan Cairns and Cynthia Williams, 183-230. Toronto: University of Toronto Press, 1985.
–. "Atomism." In *Philosophy and the Human Sciences: Philosophical Papers 2,* 187-210. Cambridge: Cambridge University Press, 1985.
–. "Foucault on Freedom and Truth." *Political Theory* 12, 2 (May 1984).
–. *The Malaise of Modernity.* Concord, ON: Anansi, 1991.
–. "The Motivation behind a Procedural Ethics." In *Kant and Political Philosophy: The Contemporary Legacy,* ed. Ronald Beiner and William James Booth, 337-60. New Haven: Yale University Press, 1993.
–. "The Politics of Recognition." In *Multiculturalism: Examining the Politics of Recognition,* ed. Amy Gutmann, 25-73. Princeton: Princeton University Press, 1994.
–. *Reconciling the Solitudes: Essays on Canadian Federalism and Nationalism,* ed. Guy Laforest. Montreal and Kingston: McGill-Queen's University Press, 1993.
Trimble, Linda. "'Good Enough Citizens': Canadian Women and Representation in Constitutional Deliberations." *International Journal of Canadian Studies* 17 (Spring 1998): 131-56.
Trudeau, Pierre Elliott. *Conversations with Canadians.* Toronto: University of Toronto Press, 1972.
–. *Federalism and the French Canadians.* Toronto: Macmillan, 1968.
–. "A Mess That Deserves a Big NO." Toronto: Robert Davies Publishing, 1992.
–. "New Treason of the Intellectuals." In *Federalism and the French Canadians.* Toronto: Macmillan, 1968.
–. "Statement to the House of Commons." House of Commons. *Debates.* 8 October 1971.
Tully, James. "Diversity's Gambit Declined." In *Constitutional Predicament: Canada after the Referendum of 1992,* ed. Curtis Cook. Montreal and Kingston: McGill-Queen's University Press, 1994.
–. *Strange Multiplicity: Constitutionalism in an Age of Diversity.* Cambridge: Cambridge University Press, 1995.

–, ed. *Philosophy in an Age of Pluralism: The Philosophy of Charles Taylor in Question.* Cambridge: Cambridge University Press, 1994.
Turpel, Mary Ellen. "Aboriginal Peoples and the Canadian Charter: Interpretive Monopolies, Cultural Differences." In *Canadian Human Rights Yearbook, 1989-91,* 3-45.
–. "The Charlottetown Discord and Aboriginal Peoples' Struggles for Fundamental Political Change." In *The Charlottetown Accord, the Referendum, and the Future of Canada,* ed. Kenneth McRoberts and Patrick Monahan. Toronto: University of Toronto Press, 1993.
Ujimoto, K. Victor. "Multiculturalism and the Global Information Society." In *Deconstructing a Nation: Immigration, Multiculturalism and Racism in '90s Canada,* ed. Vic Satzewich. Halifax: Fernwood Publishing, 1992.
Venne, Michel, ed. *Vive Quebec! New Thinking and New Approaches to the Quebec Nation,* trans. Robert Chodos and Louisa Blair. Toronto: James Lorimer and Company, 2001.
Vipond, Robert. "From Provincial Autonomy to Provincial Equality (Or, Clyde Wells and the Distinct Society)." In *Is Quebec Nationalism Just? Perspectives from Anglophone Canada,* ed. Joseph Carens. Montreal and Kingston: McGill-Queen's University Press, 1995.
Vosko, Leah F. "The Pasts (and Futures) of Feminist Political Economy in Canada: Reviving the Debate." In *Studies in Political Economy: Developments in Feminism,* ed. Caroline Andrew, Pat Armstrong, Hugh Armstrong, Wallace Clement, and Leah F. Vosko. Toronto: Women's Press, 2003.
Weaver, Sally M. *Making Canadian Indian Policy: The Hidden Agenda, 1968-1970.* Toronto: University of Toronto Press, 1981.
–. "Segregation and the Indian Act: The Dialogue of Equality vs. Special Status." In *Identities: The Impact of Ethnicity on Canadian Society,* ed. Wsevolod W. Isajiw. Canadian Ethnic Studies Association series, vol. 5. Toronto: P. Martin Associates, 1977.
Webber, Jeremy. *Reimagining Canada: Language, Culture, Community, and the Canadian Constitution.* Montreal and Kingston: McGill-Queen's University Press, 1994.
Whitaker, Reg. "The Dog That Never Barked: Who Killed Asymmetrical Federalism?" In *The Charlottetown Accord, the Referendum, and the Future of Canada,* ed. Kenneth McRoberts and Patrick Monahan. Toronto: University of Toronto Press, 1993.
–. *The End of Privacy: How Total Surveillance Is Becoming a Reality.* New York: The New Press, 1999.
–. "Sovereign Division: Quebec Nationalism Between Liberalism and Ethnicity." In *Clash of Identities: Essays on Media, Manipulation, and Politics of the Self,* ed. James Littleton, 73-87. Toronto: Prentice Hall, 1996.
–. *A Sovereign Idea: Essays on Canada As a Democratic Community.* Montreal and Kingston: McGill-Queen's University Press, 1992.
–. "With or without Quebec?" In *"English Canada" Speaks Out,* ed. J.L. Granatstein and Kenneth McNaught, 17-29. Toronto: Doubleday Canada, 1991.
Wiseman, Nelson. "A Note on 'Hartz-Horowitz at Twenty': The Case of French Canada." *Canadian Journal of Political Science* 21 (December 1988): 795-806.
Young, Iris Marion. *Justice and the Politics of Difference.* Princeton: Princeton University Press, 1990.
–. "Unruly Categories; A Critique of Nancy Fraser's Dual Systems Theory." *New Left Review* 222 (1997): 147-60.
Žižek, Slavoj. "Multiculturalism, or, the Cultural Logic of Multinational Capitalism." *New Left Review* 225 (1997): 28-51.

Index

Aboriginal peoples, 9-10; assimilation of, 68, 70, 72; and Charlottetown Accord, 10, 85; as "citizens plus," 66-8, 73; citizenship for, 66, 68, 69, 71, 76, 79; as collectivist, 29; as communitarian, 51; culture of, 71, 74; deep diversity and, 40, 42; demand for recognition, 96; difference of, 49, 50, 71; differentiation of, 65-6, 72, 76, 78; English Canadians and, 56-7, 58; equal treatment for, 69, 71, 72; legal distinction from non-Aboriginals, 69-70, 72-3; in multicultural mosaic, 71; as nation, 9; nationalist space within Canada, 52; and polarization of unity question, 80; rejection of White Paper, 73-4; relations with non-Aboriginals, 76, 78; self-government, 10, 74, 76, 77-8, 79; separatism, 79, 80; socioeconomic conditions, 66, 67, 72; treaties, 74; unity of, 76; women, 87-8. *See also* Native Women's Association of Canada (NWAC)
Abu-Laban, Yasmeen, and Christina Gabriel, 6
Ajzenstat, Janet, 30-1, 35
Allen, Lillian, 81, 83-4
Angus, Ian, 6, 56, 60, 63
Assembly of First Nations, 50, 85
assimilation, 16, 18, 22, 68, 70, 71, 72
asymmetrical federalism, 9, 39, 41, 50-1; Calgary Declaration and, 53; and Charlottetown Accord, 43; deep diversity and, 63; English Canada and, 59; multinationalism and, 58; pan-Canadian nationalism versus, 58

Bakan, Joel, 6
Banneiji, Himani, 6
Balthazar, Louis, 35
Barry, Brian, 7
belonging, 10, 24; asymmetrical patterns of, 40; deep diversity and, 42; hierarchy of, 52; plurality of ways of, 53; in White Paper, 72-3
Benhabib, Seyla, 7
Bentham, Jeremy, 11, 98
Berger, Thomas, 34
Bhabha, Homi, 98
Bibby, Reginald, 94
bilingualism, 33, 59
Bissoondath, Neil, 94, 95
Bliss, Michael, 77
Bloc Québécois, 41
Bouchard, Lucien, 16, 39, 46, 50
Bourassa, Robert, 85
Brubaker, Rogers, 44, 105

Cairns, Alan, 65, 66, 68, 70, 78-80, 90
Calgary Declaration, 9, 16-17, 26, 40, 46-57
Callwood, June, 88-9
Campbell, Kim, 43-4
Canadian conversation, 4, 6, 45, 82; agreement on identities in, 107; agreement versus disagreement in, 26; civilizing effects of, 11, 26, 91; difference and diversity in, 22; English Canadian nationalism and,

137

59; inclusivity of, 82; line-drawing contests in, 93; logic of, 14-15, 19-20, 24, 25; majoritarian concerns in, 15; as model of "new" constitutionalism, 8, 14; national identity in, 17; nationalism in, 37; normalization of, 26; normalizing power of, 11; philosophical character, 7; polarization in, 7, 8, 14, 19-20, 23, 24-5, 29-30, 45, 60; preoccupation with unity and cohesion, 19, 26-7; two "solitudes" and, 38

"The 'Canadian' Diversity Model," 92

Canadian mosaic. *See* multicultural, mosaic

Canadian School, 6-8, 23, 105

Cardinal, Harold. *The Unjust Society*, 74

Carens, Joseph, 6, 35

Carney, Pat, 83

Chambers, Simone, 7, 8, 13, 14, 18-19, 34, 81-2, 86, 90, 91

Charlottetown Accord, 10, 43-4, 91, 106; Aboriginal peoples in, 85; Aboriginal self-government in, 76-7; asymmetry and, 43, 53; Canada clause, 43, 85; distinct society and, 47; diversity and, 82, 90; gender representation and, 83; inclusivity in, 84-6; symmetry in, 43-4; women in, 85-6, 91

Charter of Rights and Freedoms: Aboriginal peoples and, 66, 76; communitarian versus procedural liberalism and, 34, 35-6; effects of, 28-9; English Canadians and, 37; equality clause, 34; as forum for discussion, 38; individual versus collective rights in, 8, 34; limits in, 95; nationalism and, 29, 30, 37; nondiscrimination clause, 34; notwithstanding clause, 35; patriotism, 29, 34; Quebec and, 29, 30, 34, 37, 59; uniform application of, 36-7

Chrétien, Jean: on Calgary Declaration, 50; on Nunavut, 78; and White Paper, 68, 69, 72

"citizens plus," 9-10, 66-8, 73, 74-5; "citizens equal" versus, 10, 78, 79; and hierarchy of difference, 78-9

"Citizens Plus," Red Paper, 73-6

citizenship: Aboriginal peoples and, 66, 69, 71, 76, 79; differential treatment in, 31-2; differentiated, 4, 6-7, 10, 23, 31, 61; equal (*see* equal citizenship); equal treatment and, 73; federalism and, 51-2; good versus bad, 91; multicultural, 101; symmetrical, 58

civic republicanism, 30

Clark, Glen, 47

Clark, Joe, 84, 85, 89

Code, Lorraine, 20

cohesion, 13, 61, 63; differentiation and, 73; diversity and, 26-7; national, 18; nondiscrimination and, 36; in White Paper, 72-3

collectivism, individualism versus, 8, 29-31, 34, 35

communitarian liberalism, 32; procedural liberalism versus, 31-4, 36-7; in Quebec, 30, 33

communitarianism: of Aboriginal peoples, 51; liberalism versus, 30; provincial equality and, 46; in Quebec, 51

Constitution: 1982 Act, 40; agreement on, 45

constitutional patriotism, 18

constitutionalism, "new." *See* Chambers, Simone

Cook, Ramsay, 29, 35-6

counternationalism, 75-6

coveillance. *See* multicultural panopticism

Crispo, John, 89

Crosbie, John, 86

culture: economics versus, 20-1; equality and, 71-2; preservation of, 45; and provincial equality, 45

cultures: equal worth of, 97; fusion of horizons and, 97-8; intercultural understanding, 25-6; interpretation of, 97; respect for, 96-7

Day, Richard, 6

decentralization: of federation, 44; and symmetry, 59

deep diversity, 8-9, 23, 39-40, 41-2, 45; asymmetrical federalism and, 53, 63; clarity and, 52; fragmentation and,

Index

61; groups and, 42; national question and, 45; as reframing of problem, 45; uniqueness and, 57; unity and, 40
democracy, 90; consociational, 93; deliberative, 82
democratic legitimacy, 45
Department of Indian Affairs and Northern Development (DIAND), 67, 69, 73
dichotomies, 4, 20-1
difference(s), 6; of Aboriginal peoples, 71; in Canadian conversation, 22; categories of, 24; civilization of, 78, 82; and closure of identity, 24; dilemmas of, 10, 87; equal treatment and, 72; equality and, 20-1, 21-2, 23, 24, 74; essentialism and, 23-4; fragmentation and, 22; hierarchy within, 78-9; homogenization of, 32; identity politics and, 23; illiberalism and, 10; multiculturalism policy and, 95-6; politics of, 31; in White Paper, 71
differentiation, 31-2; of Aboriginal peoples, 65-6, 71, 76, 78; in Charter of Rights and Freedoms, 76; "citizens plus" and, 67-8; of citizenship, 61; cohesion and, 73; English Canadian rejection of, 36; on legal grounds, 72-3; and socioeconomic disadvantage, 70
Dion, Stéphane, 50
disabilities, people with, 84
distinct society clause (DSC), 33, 34-5, 36, 41, 43, 79
disunities, 89; national, 23-4
diversity, 6, 15-16; acceptance of, 53; assimilation of, 16, 18, 22; as asymmetrical difference, 22; blindness, 25; in Calgary Declaration, 49; in Canadian conversation, 14, 22; cementing of, 18; cohesion and, 26-7; as differentiation, 22; embrace of, 16-17, 19, 56; in English Canada, 63; equal citizenship and, 72; equal treatment of, 49; equality and, 22, 71; fragmentation and, 8; as gift, 16-17, 56-7; and "good life," 33; governmental scrutiny of, 100-1; liberal contradictions over, 26;

limits to, 92, 95, 96; new constitutionalism and, 14; within representation, 90; toleration and, 98; and uniformity of belonging, 52-3; unity and, 3, 7, 8, 15-16, 19, 26, 50, 63, 92
Duara, Prasenjit, 3
Durham Report, 16, 65, 70
Dworkin, Ronald, 32, 36

Eberts, Mary, 85
economics, culture versus, 20-1
English Canada: accommodation of Quebec, 62; asymmetry and, 59; authenticity of, 60, 62; and Charter of Rights and Freedoms, 37; and distinct society clause, 33; diversity in, 63; equality and nationalism in, 26; equality discourse in, 36; as individualist, 8, 29-30; nationalism of, 56, 57, 58-9, 61-2, 63-4; nonidentity of, 62; as partnership of nations, 57; procedural liberalism in, 29-30, 33; proceduralism in, 32-3; and Quebec as distinct nation, 57-8; self-consciousness of, 60; self-recognition of, 57; unity of, 63
English Canadians: and Aboriginal peoples, 58; and Charter proceduralism, 34-5; common interests of, 62, 63; and distinct society clause, 34-5, 36; embrace of Quebec, 59; equal recognition for, 52; equality and, 58; identity of, 58, 61-2, 63; as liberal-individualists, 51; and multinationalism, 58, 62; pan-Canadianism of, 9, 57, 60, 61-2; provincial equality and, 45-6, 51, 52, 58; on purpose of Canada, 32; rejection of differentiation, 36; resentment of, 45-6, 62; symmetry of views, 50-1, 53; uniformity of belonging, 52-3
equal citizenship, 3-4, 21-3, 25, 73; for Aboriginal peoples, 66, 71, 76; and Calgary Declaration, 46-8; differentiated versus, 31; diversity and, 72; provincial equality and, 51-2; self-governance and, 76
equal treatment, 36; for Aboriginal peoples, 69, 71, 72; citizenship and,

Index

73; difference and, 72; discrimination and, 31; and diversity, 49; equality and, 70; justice and, 70; unity through, 63

equality, 10, 12; in Calgary Declaration, 49; clause in Charter of Rights and Freedoms, 34; culture and, 71-2; difference and, 20-2, 23, 24, 74; diversity and, 22, 71; English Canadians and, 58; equal treatment and, 70; freedom through, 32; gender, 83-4, 88-9; imposition of, 24; liberal contradictions over, 26; nationalism and, 26; of provinces (*see* provincial equality); uniqueness and, 49; unity and, 24

equality discourse: and clarity, 52; in English Canada, 36; procedural liberalism and, 36; as recognition claim, 51; unity and, 36-7

essentialism, 6; of differences, 23-4

ethnic groups, uniqueness of, 49

exclusion, 16; disability and, 84; inclusion versus, 87

federalism: asymmetrical (*see* asymmetrical federalism); citizenship and, 51-2; division of powers, 44; multinational, 61; procedural versus communitarian liberalism and, 33; symmetrical, 56, 58

Feld, John, 84

feminist theory: and equality versus difference, 20-1

Flanagan, Tom. *First Nations? Second Thoughts*, 78

Fontaine, Phil, 50

Foucault, Michel, 11, 52, 93, 98-100

fragmentation: agreement versus, 25; in Canadian conversation, 18, 25, 26; deep diversity and, 61; difference and, 22; diversity and, 8, 90; English Canadians and, 63; national question and, 106

Fraser, Nancy, 20-1

free trade, 59

freedom: liberal governance and, 100; power through, 99, 100; through equality, 32

French language, 33

gender equality, 83-4, 88-9
Gordon, Colin, 100
governmentality, 10, 99-100
Grant, Wendy, 87-8
groups: conflict among, 93; deep diversity and, 42; dominant, 103-4; ethnic, 49; minority (*see* minorities/minority groups); recognition of, 96, 97, 103-4; self-government versus representation, 90; special interest, 86, 89; underrepresented, 90, 91; women's, 10, 82. *See also* National Action Committee on the Status of Women; Native Women's Association of Canada

Gutmann, Amy, 7
Gwyn, Richard, 62, 94, 95

Habermas, Jürgen, 14, 18, 28-9
Harcourt, Mike, 83
Harper, Stephen, 78
Harris, Mike, 48
Hartz, Louis, 30, 31
Hawthorn Report, 9-10, 65-8, 71, 72, 73, 74, 78, 79
Hegel, Georg Wilhelm Friedrich, 31
Herder, Johann Gottfried von, 31
hierarchy, 26, 32; of belonging, 52; difference within, 78-9
Hindess, Barry, 100
homogeneity, 31
Honig, Bonnie, 13, 15, 24, 26-7
Horowitz, Gad, 30, 31
hybridity, 6, 102

identity/identities, 6; agreement on, in Canadian conversation, 107; clash of, 26; construction of, 6; difference and, 23; of English Canadians, 58, 61-2, 63; formed by recognition, 97; logic of, 6, 9, 107; of minority groups, 96; misrecognition of, 93; politics, 6, 94; shared, 61; totalizing of, 23-4

Ignatieff, Michael, 7; on the Charter of Rights and Freedoms, 34, 38; on group versus individual rights, 29; on participation of groups, 82; on

recognition as two-way street, 57; on "rights revolution," 28-9; on self-recognition of English Canada, 57; on symmetrical federalism, 56
illiberalism: difference and, 10; and minority groups, 96; Quebec's non-embrace of Charter as, 37
inclusivity: of Canadian conversation, 82; in Charlottetown negotiations, 84-6; exclusion versus, 87
Indian Act, 67, 69, 74, 75
Indian Chiefs of Alberta. "Citizens Plus," 74-5
individualism: collectivism versus, 8, 29-31, 34, 35; of equality strategies, 22

justice, 10, 12; equal treatment and, 70; goal-based versus rights-based theories, 36; liberal contradictions over, 26; national contestation in terms of, 38; socioeconomic, 20

Kant, Immanuel, 32
Klein, Ralph, 47
Kymlicka, Will, 6, 14, 63; on Aboriginal differentiation, 78; on distinction between self-government and representation, 90; on English Canadian nationalism, 9, 58-9, 62; *Finding Our Way*, 56, 105; *Multicultural Citizenship*, 105; on multicultural citizenship, 7; on multiculturalism policy, 10-11, 94, 95-6; on pan-Canadian nationalism, 56, 61-2; and symmetry/asymmetry divide, 60-1; theory of multicultural citizenship, 23; on unity among nations of Canada, 60-1

Laforest, Guy, 35, 60
languages: equal access to French, 33
LaSelva, Samuel, 33, 90
Laurendeau, André, 59
liberal governance, 100, 101
liberalism: civic republicanism versus, 30; communitarian versus procedural, 30, 32-4, 36-7; limits to, 92-6, 102-3
Locke, John, 29, 31

McDonough, Alexa, 83
Mackey, Eva, 6
Macklem, Patrick, 78
McLachlin, Beverley, 38, 78
McRoberts, Kenneth, 25, 35, 60
Mahoney, Kathleen, 88
Mann, Steven, 99
Manning, Preston, 47, 48, 49, 86
Mansbridge, Peter, 76, 88
Meech Lake Accord, 40-1, 82, 106; Aboriginal issues excluded from, 76; Charlottetown campaign compared with, 85; distinct society clause, 33, 35, 47, 53; English Canadian opposition to, 35; symmetry of, 40-1
Mercredi, Ovide, 85
Miller, J.R., 75
Milne, David, 41
minorities/minority groups, 10; civilizing of, 11; and embrace of diversity, 17; marginalization of, 94; restrictions on, 94; traditional practices, 96
Minow, Martha, 10, 87
misrecognition, 10, 97, 103-4; of identities, 93. *See also* recognition
multicultural: citizenship, 101; gaze, 101, 103; governance, 100-1; mosaic, 24, 40, 71, 98; nationalism, 5-6, 15, 26
multicultural panopticism, 98-102; and coveillance, 99, 101
multiculturalism, 5, 59; English-Canadian nationality and, 63; limits to, 11, 94, 95
multiculturalism policy, 98; difference and, 94-6; limits within, 10-11, 95-6
multinational federalism, 61
multinationalism, 9; asymmetry and, 58; English Canadians and, 58, 62

National Action Committee on the Status of Women (NAC), 10, 85-6, 86-7, 88, 89, 91, 116n32
national: disunities, 23-4; identity, 14, 17-18
National Indian Brotherhood, 74, 75
nationalism(s), 5; in Canadian conversation, 14, 37; Charter of Rights and

Freedoms and, 29, 30, 37; clash of, 26, 55; competing, 9; debate, 26; differentiated citizenship among, 61; of English Canada, 9, 56, 57, 58-9, 61-2, 63-4; equality and, 26; ethnic, 37; line drawing in, 93; multicultural, 15, 26; national difference and, 38; pan-Canadian, 9, 55-6, 57, 58, 60, 61-2; provincial equality and, 57; relational nature, 5; relations with Canada, 60-1; unity and, 106

Native Women's Association of Canada (NWAC), 85, 87-8

Newfoundland government website, on Quebec in Calgary Declaration, 49

Nielsen, Jim, 43-4

Nisga'a Treaty, 66, 78

nondiscrimination, 31, 32; clause in Charter, 34; cohesion and, 36; and individual rights, 33; unity and, 36

Nunavut, 66, 78, 106

Oka crisis, 76

pan-Canadian nationalism, 9, 55-6, 57, 58, 60, 61-2

panopticism. *See* multicultural panopticism

Parekh, Bhiku, 7, 17, 101

participation, civilizing effect of, 82

polarization: in Canadian conversation, 14, 19-20, 23, 24-5, 29-30, 45, 60; of political choices, 23; unity and, 80

procedural communitarianism, 46

procedural liberalism, 32; communitarian versus, 31-4, 36-7; in English Canada, 29-30, 33; equality discourse and, 36; purpose of, 36; unity and, 36

proceduralism: of Charter of Rights and Freedoms, 34; in English Canada, 32-3; in United States, 32

provinces, uniqueness of, 9, 49, 50

provincial equality, 8, 9; asymmetrical federalism versus, 39, 50-1; and Calgary Declaration, 46-7; communitarianism and, 46; and cultural preservation, 45; English Canadians and, 51, 52, 58; equal citizenship and, 51-2; as misconceiving Canada, 25; nationalism and, 57; Quebec as distinct versus, 43-4; resentment within, 45-6

Quebec: 1995 referendum, 19, 46, 106; "appeasing" of, 48; Bill 178, 35; and Charter of Rights and Freedoms, 29, 30, 37; as collectivist, 29; as communitarian, 51; communitarian liberalism in, 8, 30, 33; cultural survival, 32, 33; deep diversity and, 40; as distinct nation, 57-8; as distinct society, 8-9, 33, 34, 36, 39, 40, 41, 43, 47, 49, 50-1, 79; embraced by English Canadians, 59; English language minority in, 35; language laws, 35; liberalism of, 8, 37-8; nationalism, 37, 55; and pan-Canadianism, 9, 56, 60; recognition for, 39, 96; special treatment for, 47, 48; unique character, 47, 48, 49; use of notwithstanding clause, 35

Québécois: deep diversity and, 42; English Canadian embrace of diversity and, 56-7; nationalist space within Canada, 52; on purpose of Canada, 32

racism, 16

Rae, Bob, 84, 85

Rawls, John, 32, 36

Razack, Sherene, 6

Rebick, Judy, 85-6, 86-7, 91

recognition: within Canadian conversation, 14; clash of collective demands, 51; deep diversity and, 42; equal, 31-2; equality discourse and, 51; of groups, 96, 97; and identity, 6, 97; line drawing in, 93; nationalist, 6; opposition to demands, 51; redistribution versus, 20-1; struggles, 10, 14, 25; of value of different cultures, 97. *See also* misrecognition

Red Paper. *See* "Citizens Plus"

referendums, 87. *See also* Charlottetown Accord

Reform Party, 24, 41, 47-8, 50, 76

representation: diversity within, 90; partiality versus impartiality of, 10, 87-9, 91; self-government versus, 90; within Senate, 83-4; unity and, 90
Resnick, Philip, 9, 56, 62, 63
rhizomatic politics, 107
Rousseau, Jean-Jacques, 27, 29, 31, 32, 36
Royal Commission on Aboriginal Peoples, 66, 77-8, 123n36
Royal Commission on Bilingualism and Biculturalism, 94
Russell, Peter, 13

Sanders, Douglas, 76
Saskatchewan government website: on Quebec in Calgary Declaration, 48, 49
Schlesinger Jr., Arthur, 18
Schlesinger, Joe, 84
Schwartz, Brian, 44
Scott, Ian, 76
Scott, Joan W., 21-2, 23
Smith, Peter, 30-1
sovereignty, 99-100
"special" interest groups, 86, 89
"special" treatment: for Aboriginal peoples, 70; for Quebec, 34, 47, 48
Speirs, Rosemary, 47
substantive liberalism. *See* communitarian liberalism
Supreme Court of Canada, 35
symmetry: asymmetry versus, 61; in Charlottetown Accord, 43-4; decentralization and, 59; of English Canadian view, 50-1, 53; of equality strategies, 22-3; of federalism, 56; of Meech Lake Accord, 40-1; and Quebec as distinct society, 41

Taylor, Charles, 6, 7; on Canadian "people," 14; on deep diversity, 8, 23, 39-40, 41-2, 52; on difference between political cultures of Quebec and English Canada, 35; on English Canadian uniformity of belonging, 52-3; equality/difference dichotomy and, 20-1; on fragmentation, 61; Hegelianism of, 121n24; on individual versus collective rights, 29-30; on limits to diversity, 92; *The Malaise of Modernity*, 105; on misrecognition, 103; neo-Kantian interpretation, 32; participation in Canadian conversation, 37; on plurality of ways of belonging, 53; "The Politics of Recognition," 31-2, 96-8; on procedural versus communitarian liberalism, 31-4, 36-7; on proceduralism of Charter, 34-5; on Quebec/English Canada divide, 37-8, 51; on Quebec's status for, 34; on recognition of Quebec, 51, 57-8; on reconciliation of solitudes, 8; Rousseauian interpretation, 32; "Shared and Divergent Values," 32-4
Tobin, Brian, 48
Toryism, and socialism, 30
transformative politics, 27, 91
Trimble, Linda, 90-1
Trudeau, Pierre: and Aboriginal peoples, 70; and Canadian School, 7; and Charlottetown Accord, 43, 86; "Citizens Plus" presented to, 74; death of, 106; multiculturalism policy, 92, 94, 98; pan-Canadian nationalism of, 55-6, 59-60; and provincial equality, 22, 25; and Quebec nationalism, 55; and White Paper, 72, 75, 93
Tully, James, 7, 14, 39, 78, 105; on diversity blindness, 25; on recognition of cultural diversity, 23; on White Paper, 70
Turpel, Mary Ellen, 75, 76

uniqueness: of Aboriginal peoples, 49, 50; deep diversity and, 57; equality and, 49; of provinces, 49, 50
United States: culture wars, 4; feminism in, 20; proceduralism in, 32; unitary constitutional model, 14
unity, 14; of Aboriginal peoples, 76; among Canadian nations, 61; deep diversity and, 40; and democratic governance, 79; distinctness and, 49;

diversity and, 3, 7, 8, 15-16, 19, 26, 50, 56, 63, 92; of English Canada, 63; and equal treatment, 63; equality and, 24, 36-7; as fantasy, 105; as illusion, 25; imperative, 15, 18-20, 24; imposition of, 24; majoritarian vantage point on, 79-80; nationalism and, 106; nondiscrimination and, 36; in opposition, 4; polarization and, 80; procedural liberalism and, 36; representation and, 90; shared identity and, 61; unitary vision versus, 18-19

"We the people," 8, 10, 14, 19, 91
Weaver, Sally, 68-9, 75
Webb, Karen, 88
Webber, Jeremy, 7, 14, 24-5, 61

Wells, Clyde, 39
Western provinces, 40, 41
Whitaker, Reg, 59, 60, 63, 126n22
White Paper on "Indian policy," 9, 16, 65, 68-73, 74, 75, 76, 78
Wilson, Gordon, 76
women: Aboriginal, 87-8; in Charlottetown Accord, 85-6, 91; groups, 10, 82 (*see also* National Action Committee on the Status of Women; Native Women's Association of Canada); underrepresentation of, 83, 87, 91

Young, Iris Marion, 28

Žižek, Slavoj, 56

Gerald Kernerman
Multicultural Nationalism: Civilizing Difference, Constituting Community (2005)

Pamela A. Jordan
Defending Rights in Russia: Lawyers, the State, and Legal Reform in the Post-Soviet Era (2005)

Anna Pratt
Securing Borders: Detention and Deportation in Canada (2005)

Kirsten Johnson Kramar
Unwilling Mothers, Unwanted Babies: Infanticide in Canada (2005)

W.A. Bogart
Good Government? Good Citizens? Courts, Politics, and Markets in a Changing Canada (2005)

Catherine Dauvergne
Humanitarianism, Identity, and Nation: Migration Laws of Australia and Canada (2005)

Michael Lee Ross
First Nations Sacred Sites in Canada's Courts (2005)

Andrew Woolford
Between Justice and Certainty: Treaty Making in British Columbia (2005)

John McLaren, Andrew Buck, and Nancy Wright (eds.)
Despotic Dominion: Property Rights in British Settler Societies (2004)

Georges Campeau
From UI to EI: Waging War on the Welfare State (2004)

Alvin J. Esau
The Courts and the Colonies: The Litigation of Hutterite Church Disputes (2004)

Christopher N. Kendall
Gay Male Pornography: An Issue of Sex Discrimination (2004)

Roy B. Flemming
Tournament of Appeals: Granting Judicial Review in Canada (2004)

Constance Backhouse and Nancy L. Backhouse
The Heiress vs the Establishment: Mrs. Campbell's Campaign for Legal Justice (2004)

Christopher P. Manfredi
Feminist Activism in the Supreme Court: Legal Mobilization and the Women's Legal Education and Action Fund (2004)

Annalise Acorn
Compulsory Compassion: A Critique of Restorative Justice (2004)

Jonathan Swainger and Constance Backhouse (eds.)
People and Place: Historical Influences on Legal Culture (2003)

Jim Phillips and Rosemary Gartner
Murdering Holiness: The Trials of Franz Creffield and George Mitchell (2003)

David R. Boyd
Unnatural Law: Rethinking Canadian Environmental Law and Policy (2003)

Ikechi Mgbeoji
Collective Insecurity: The Liberian Crisis, Unilateralism, and Global Order (2003)

Rebecca Johnson
Taxing Choices: The Intersection of Class, Gender, Parenthood, and the Law (2002)

John McLaren, Robert Menzies, and Dorothy E. Chunn (eds.)
Regulating Lives: Historical Essays on the State, Society, the Individual, and the Law (2002)

Joan Brockman
Gender in the Legal Profession: Fitting or Breaking the Mould (2001)

Printed and bound in Canada by Friesens
Set in Scala and MetaPlus by Artegraphica Design Co. Ltd.
Copyeditor: Sarah Wight
Proofreader: Gail Copeland
Indexer: Noeline Bridge